REVISED EDITION

IN THE BEGINNING
GENESIS 1-11

JANICE BOBANIS

WESTBOW
PRESS®
A DIVISION OF THOMAS NELSON
& ZONDERVAN

WestBow Press books may be ordered through booksellers or by contacting:

WestBow Press
A Division of Thomas Nelson & Zondervan
1663 Liberty Drive
Bloomington, IN 47403
www.westbowpress.com
844-714-3454

For more information, go to http://www.JaniceBobanis.com

Facebook: Janice Bobanis/Christian Author & Speaker
Instagram: janicebobanistcm

ISBN: 978-1-6642-9276-5 (sc)
ISBN: 978-1-6642-9277-2 (hc)
ISBN: 978-1-6642-9278-9 (e)

Library of Congress Control Number: 2023903372

Print information available on the last page.

WestBow Press rev. date: 02/27/2023

It doesn't matter what we think;
it only matters what God says about it!
—Janice Bobanis

Contents

Dedication

This Genesis study is dedicated with love and appreciation to my Bible study ladies! You have been my students, my prayer warriors, and my encouragement for so many years. I love you to the moon and back!

Anita G.
Ann F.
Bev S.
Carolyn M.
Cynthia C.
Daphne F.
Darlene B.
Debbie V.
Gale B.
Jan W.
Kathleen C.
Laurel O.
Lindsey H.
Missy S.
Patti C.
Paula L.
Paula P.

Sheri H.
Sheryl R.
Stacey B.
Wanda B.

I also want to thank my sweet family for allowing me to fulfill my calling. You have sacrificed time and attention over the years, and I am grateful you have put up with me through it all.

Thank you, Jeff, Caroline, and Claire! I love you very much!

What Readers Are Saying

"Many people feel the Old Testament is a dusty, old book that is not worthy of notice. Janice's passion for the Word brought Genesis to life for me. In a world where truth is in short supply, you'll find it here and learn how relevant and applicable it is for us today. I loved this study!!" –Sheryl R.

"A great Bible study for the new Christian. Concise, simplified, and explained God's laws on plants, genetically modified foods and interbreeding of animals. Kept interest at a peak!" –Laurel O.

"This Bible study gives a fresh look at God's original blueprint for our lives today. In depth, yet easy to understand; this Bible study is so applicable. I highly recommend it." –Debbie V.

"Love this book! Brings me great satisfaction every time I read a new chapter and reflect on how the chapter actually refers to my life. A great way to actively read the Bible and get back to God!"–Gray

"Is discomfort in your body about the direction of the world? Do you lie awake wondering why honest values, community, integrity leadership, and physical health seem to be withering away? This book will help you find the root of many of those concerns, and may even inspire actions that you may have never thought you had in you.

The conclusions reached and so beautifully organized by Janice Bobanis are not for the "feel good" Sunday school class. Prepare yourself to go deep into the oldest truths in written text. These truths expose the lost hope in the systems created by man and begin to remove the debris from the trail back home.

For me, personally, I found Bobanis's approach to Noah the most reassuring. She confirmed for me that others have "heard/felt" God's wisdom and have had the faith to act on that wisdom. I did not realize that Noah had worked on the ark for 120 years before the first rains. All but EIGHT people called him crazy. Can you imagine how hard that must have been? Lonely, physically difficult, and mentally exhausting for a period longer than a modern lifespan. Clearly, a level of faith not known today.

I encourage everyone to dive deep into the Old Testament with this book as your guide."–Spencer M.

"Great teachings! So many people don't talk about the truth that Janice talks about in "In the Beginning." I highly recommend doing this with a small group."–Claire G.

Introduction

I hope you are as excited as I am about this study! You are going to feel informed and blessed by what you learn. I wrote this study for my small group. After we finished the semester, I asked the attendees what they thought about it. They loved it so much they encouraged me to publish it.

You are going to learn surprising truths about God's creation. You will find so many ways this study is applicable to your everyday life. I guarantee you will be talking about what you learn with your friends. It is different from anything you have ever done. It is detailed without being tedious.

The Old Testament is a treasure trove of life-changing application. It is very relevant and should never be discounted as outdated. My students have come to love how I teach it because I make it simple to understand yet intellectually stimulating.

Learn what happens when we mess with God's creation. Know and understand what is going on with our food supply. Develop principles that will strengthen your marriage. Learn some valuable tips on work ethics from Genesis 1. Find out what scripture says regarding our most controversial social issues. Gain a new perspective on God's timetable as we study about Noah. The list goes on and on!

If you grew up in the church, you may have been tossed around the Bible. In this study, you will get a better understanding of how God's plan unfolds from Genesis to Revelation. I like to weave in the New Testament from time to time to show how it all fits together.

I encourage my students to insert themselves in the story. None of the people we will study were perfect. Pay attention to their experiences and how the Lord interacts with them.

My intention is to lead you to the biblical answers. Please refer to the Message from the Author for further insight and explanation on the lessons. You will find these at the end of the group of lessons it covers. It is my greatest desire for you to finish this study feeling like your time was well spent. I hope you walk away at the end feeling inspired, informed, and hungering for more!

How to Use This Bible Study

Individual Study

If you choose to do this study by yourself rather than in a group setting, I encourage you to only do one lesson a day. You could even do one lesson a week if you wanted to. This allows you to digest the application of the lesson. It's important to ponder and apply what you are learning. Think of it as savoring a wonderful meal. Eating slow, savoring each bite, and enjoying fellowship through conversation makes for a great dining experience! So, chew on each question, savor the commentary, and have a great conversation with the Lord through your study! This is a healthier way to take in God's Word. Don't look at getting your lesson done as something to check off your to-do list. Rather, look at it as a time of refreshment, rejuvenation, and personal growth!

Group Study

You may choose to do this as a small-group study with your neighbors, a Sunday school class, or a group of friends. I suggest keeping your group to about fifteen people. You will need a designated person to lead the group through the questions in an open discussion.

Depending on your group, you can divide up the study into whatever works best. I suggest doing no more than two lessons a week. That way, you can get through all the questions in your group discussion when you meet.

In my years of leading small groups, I found that doing a ten-week fall semester and a ten-week spring semester is very manageable. You can have your group do two lessons per week and discuss them when you meet.

On the other hand, you could divide the forty lessons into four ten-week semesters covering one lesson per week if your group wants to meet year-round. (Keep in mind that some lessons are really short and may not yield enough to discuss in one session.) You can take breaks around important holidays when everyone is busier than usual. This study can be as flexible to your group as it needs to be.

Lesson 1

Genesis 1:1–2: Who Is God?

Read Genesis 1:1–2 and pray that God will speak to you through this lesson.

Answer the following questions.

1. It's important to understand exactly who was present at creation. According to the following verses, who were the three?

Genesis 1:1

Genesis 1:2

John 1:1–2

1

2. According to John 1:14 and John 1:17, what did the "Word" later become? What was His name from which grace and truth would come?

You have just identified the Holy Trinity! Many people find the Trinity hard to comprehend, but it's easier if you think of it like this: Water comes in three forms: liquid, solid (ice), and gas (vapor). They are all forms of water, but they have different purposes. The Holy Trinity is made up of three parts: God the Father, Jesus Christ, and the Holy Spirit. They are all the same being, but they serve different purposes. God the Father is our heavenly Father. Jesus Christ is God in the flesh who came to earth to dwell among us and to die on the cross for our sins. The Holy Spirit is the Spirit of God who comes to dwell in our hearts when we become true, genuine believers. All three were present at creation. Once we become true, genuine believers, the Spirit of God, not the sinful nature, controls us. In Romans 8:8–9, Paul tells the true believers, "Those controlled by the sinful nature cannot please God. You, however, are controlled *not* by the sinful nature but by the Spirit, if the Spirit of God lives in you. And if anyone does not have the Spirit of Christ, that person does not belong to Christ."

I have taught many years of Bible study. I've witnessed many people who have sat in church their whole lives who thought they were saved, who thought they were going to heaven because they are good people. As a teacher, one of the most rewarding experiences I get to have is watching someone "get Jesus"! Folks, we will never be good enough to get to heaven on our own. We must have Jesus! So, I want you to realize that when you are doing your lesson, and your heart is pricked over some sin you are guilty of, that is the Lord lovingly tapping you on the shoulder! He wants a relationship with *you*! He wants to bless *you*! He wants to protect *you*, guide *you*, and teach *you*! So, I hope that you are drawn into this study with great interest and enthusiasm, because if you have the mindset, you are going to be blessed, changed, and left hungering for more!

3. Using the dictionary, look up the definition of these three words:

Omnipotent

Omniscient

Omnipresent

4. The three definitions above describe God, our Creator. In what area of your life or in what circumstance do you find the above description of God comforting or challenging? (See also Hebrews 4:12–13.)

I have to tell you that God's Word is extremely powerful. The Word was God and was with God in the beginning.

Then the Word became flesh (Jesus Christ). And you are studying the "Word" right now! The Bible is God's way of communicating with us.

I speak from personal experience and want to share my life-changing experience with you. Years ago, I was a young mother who had recently quit work to become a stay-at-home mother. On a limited income at the time, I decided to sell some purses a relative made at our local church bazaar. I rented a booth for one hundred dollars. I sat there for three days and didn't sell a single purse. The lady at the booth next to me said, "I can't believe you haven't sold any of those beautiful purses!"

I said, "I know! I'm in the hole one hundred dollars!"

She then said to me in a surprised and bewildered tone, "But the money goes to the church!"

And I replied, "I don't care! I'm in the hole one hundred dollars!"

Well, I was in a Bible study for the first time then, and the Monday after the church bazaar, I was doing my lesson. We were studying the book of John. I came to a question that asked me to read John 2:12–16. Jesus's words seemed to levitate off the page as I read, "Get these out of here! How dare you turn my Father's house into a market!" The scripture was about Jesus scolding the people in the temple for selling goods for profit! They were using the temple for personal gain, just as I was doing. Those words pierced my heart like a double-edged sword. Well, it was the absolute worst feeling and best feeling all at the same time. Those words identified my sin and what was separating me from an incredible fellowship with the Lord.

Friends, that's God's grace to me! For the first time in my life, I saw myself as a sinner! I had always compared myself to others and thought I was a good person, but when you compare yourself to the Word of God, it is very convicting when you fall short of it! At that very moment, what Jesus did on the cross for me made perfect sense. We cannot go to heaven on our own. We will never be perfect enough! I became a true believer because God had spoken directly to my heart and identified my sin. He truly is all-knowing, ever present, and all-powerful. When God shows us our sin, it is His grace to us because sin is what separates us from Him.

At that moment, I "got Jesus," and my life has never been the same since. So, if you are convicted while doing this Bible study, good for you! It is God's mercy, because He is showing you what is separating you from Him. The Word of God is truly a relationship book, a conversation between you and the Almighty!

5. Look up Luke 1:37 and Luke 18:27. What in your life has seemed impossible or out of reach, and how do these verses give you hope?

6. What are Matthew 17:20, Hebrews 11:1, and Hebrews 11:6 really saying about faith?

What does 1 John 5:14–15 say about prayer?

7. What did you learn that was new to you, or what stood out to you in this lesson?

Lesson 2

Genesis 1:1–2:3: God's Word Brings Change

Read Genesis 1:1–2:3 and pray that God will speak to you through this lesson.

Answer the following questions.

1. As you read Genesis 1:1–2:3, what action do you see God do to set things in motion each day?

2. God's Word changed the landscape of the universe. His Word is powerful and can speak to us as well. In what area of your life do you welcome the Word of God to bring change, understanding, and healing?

Where would you prefer to ignore the power of God's Word?

3. Starting with the first day and working through the days of creation, write down what God created each day.

First Day:

Second Day:

Third Day:

Fourth Day:

Fifth Day:

Sixth Day:

4. Each day God created, He had to "see" something before He moved on to the next part of His creation. What did He have to see on each individual day and as a whole? (See also Genesis 1:31.)

5. What does God need to see in your life before He can take you to the next step on your journey?

6. What did you learn that was new to you, or what stood out to you in this lesson?

Lesson 3

Genesis 1:20–31: Seeds and Breeds

Read Genesis 1:20–31 and pray that God will speak to you through this lesson.

Answer the following questions.

God commanded Adam to rule over the plants and animals, but He also gave boundaries to this responsibility.

1. Read Leviticus 19:19. Identify the three commands God gives us in this verse.

2. Do you believe these commands are applicable today, knowing that God saw what He had created as very good? Why?

3. Give an example of an animal that has been intentionally crossbred by humans to achieve a desired result.

4. Name a fruit or vegetable that is the result of crossing seeds of two plants to achieve a desired result.

5. Using Google or a dictionary, define the following terms.

Genetically modified organism (GMO):

Hybrid:

6. Is a dog who is considered a mutt a hybrid? Explain.

7. Thinking long term, what's the difference in a mixed breed (a mutt) and a dog that is intentionally crossbred?

8. How does Leviticus 19:19, along with the definitions of *hybrid* and *GMO*, change your views about where science is headed with plants and animals?

9. From what practical standpoint do you think our all-knowing (omniscient) God included this law in Leviticus? (You may want to look up the dangers or disadvantages of hybrid and GMO plants and animals.)

Did you know scientists have found that when we cross seeds and cross breeds, the seed or semen can eventually become sterile? There are other reasons for not cross-pollinating and crossbreeding, as well. Hmm. Maybe God is a little smarter and knows the future better than *humans*!

10. What did you learn that was new to you, or what stood out to you in this lesson?

Lesson 4

Genesis 1:26–28: God Doesn't Make Mistakes

Read Genesis 1:26–28 and pray that God will speak to you through this lesson.

Answer the following questions.

1. Read Genesis 1:26 and take notice of the words "us" and "our," which tell us God is talking with the other two parts of the Trinity about "making" humans in their image. What abilities of the senses do you think humans and the three persons of the Trinity share? Use the following verses to help you list those abilities:

Genesis 8:21:

Genesis 16:13:

Genesis 32:22–32 and 1 Samuel 10:26:

Psalm 94:9:

John 11:35:

2 Peter 1:18:

It's comforting to know that God understands us, because He has all the human senses we have.

2. Read Genesis 1:27 with Psalm 139:13–16. What do these verses say about the details of God's creation of you?

3. After reading the verses in question 2, read Deuteronomy 22:5.

Why do you think cross-dressing is so detestable to God?

Do you think God makes mistakes? Explain.

4. In light of "gender identity" issues, do you believe it is possible for our Creator to stop the confusion of someone who struggles with gender identity and give them peace

Janice Bobanis

with their birth gender? Explain your answer. (See Luke 18:27 and I Corinthians 14:33.)

5. What did you learn that was new to you or what stood out to you in this lesson?

Lesson 5

Genesis 1:27–31: Nature's Bounty

Read Genesis 1:27–31 and pray that God will speak to you through this lesson.

Answer the following questions.

1. In Genesis 1:29–30, what exactly did God allow humans and animals to eat at this particular time?

2. Read Genesis 9:1–3. After Noah and the Great Flood, what exactly did God allow humans to eat?

3. What's interesting to you about the comparison of Genesis 1:30 to Genesis 9:1–3? If you are a vegetarian, does this change your mind about being one? If so, why?

4. Something to ponder: Can you think of a reason why God would allow people to eat only vegetation *before* the

flood and not allow the eating of animals until *after* the flood?

What were our bodies initially designed to eat?

5. Referring to Daniel 1:11–20, what difference did eating only vegetables make in Daniel's life?

(Don't get me wrong, people! I am a meat and potatoes girl! However, this makes you stop and think a little bit, right?)

6. What did you learn that was new to you, or what stood out to you in this lesson?

Lesson 6

Genesis 1:1–2:3: God's Work Ethic

Read Genesis 1:1–2:3 and pray that God will speak to you through this lesson.

Answer the following questions.

1. Write down your typical weekly routine:

Monday:

Tuesday:

Wednesday:

Thursday:

Friday:

Saturday:

Sunday:

2. Read and look closely at Genesis 1:1–2:3. List some practical things you see about God's work ethic during these seven days of creation that you can apply to your own life.

3. What stands out the most to you in these verses?

Take a look at Genesis 2:19–20. Even God knows how to delegate to others!

4. What changes might you need to make to get the most productivity out of your week?

5. Looking at the seventh day, do you have a seventh day of rest? If so, how does that day look different from the other days of the week? Be specific.

If not, what *specific* changes or priorities do you need to make to be more in line with God's work ethic?

6. What did you learn that was new to you, or what stood out to you in this lesson?

Lesson 7

Genesis 1:1–2:3: Think about It!

Read Genesis 1:1–2:3 and pray that God will speak to you through this lesson.

Answer the following questions.

Many Bible scholars believe creation occurred somewhere between 4,000 BC and 10,000 BC (4,000–5,000 BC seems to be the most widely accepted view). Therefore, it is believed that creation occurred thousands, not billions, of years ago.

1. Read Genesis 1:5, 1:8, 1:13, 1:19, 1:23, and 1:31. What do these verses all have in common?

2. What do you believe is the actual time God spent on creation?

3. Using a dictionary, define *evolution*.

4. For what practical reason do you believe our omniscient (all-knowing) God may be making this point on each and every day according to the verses listed above in question 1?

We know that dinosaurs existed on earth because of fossil discoveries. However, it is absolutely clear from scripture that the animals were created on the fifth and sixth day. At the time of creation, death had not entered the world because sin had not entered the world. If death had not entered the world, then dinosaurs could not have died before the first human was created.

5. How does this fact challenge your thinking?

6. In your opinion, what do you think happened to the dinosaurs? Skim Genesis 6–8. (Consider the condition of the earth after the Great Flood of Noah's time. Also, it is helpful to research what dinosaurs ate!)

7. Reflect over the last seven lessons. What has been most encouraging, thought provoking, or convicting after doing these lessons?

8. What have you learned that you didn't know before?

9. On the following pages, read my message on lessons one through seven and write down your thoughts. What spoke to you? What challenged you or gave you inspiration? Write it down.

A Message from the Author

I don't know if you're into fashion or decorating, but something I learned from my mother was the value of classic things, whether it is a classic way of dressing or a classic way of decorating my house. A classic style is timeless. It is always relevant to the times and is never outdated.

God's Word is classic. It's always relevant and timeless in its application. So many people miss out because they believe the Old Testament is totally irrelevant. However, you are going to find out that it is quite the opposite! It is, in fact, always timely and never outdated!

We began our study of the Bible with Genesis and creation. It is the foundation and the beginning of everything. Not only did we learn about God's week of creative perfection but also our responsibility on how to care for it. In addition to this, we saw God's work ethic, something we should all apply to ourselves.

What I love about Genesis 1 is that God's voice changed the landscape of the universe. He took absolutely nothing and turned it into the heavens and the earth with absolute perfection. And He did this by speaking to it! For instance, the first day of creation God said, "Let there be light!" The second day He said, "Let there be an expanse between the waters to separate water from water." So, with each day He spoke, things happened, and real change began to occur!

Do you need help with the landscape of your life? Do you have situations in your life you wish were different from how they are? Maybe your marriage is in trouble, or your work situation is undesirable. Maybe your kids are giving you problems! Is there a relationship in your life that needs repair? The landscape of your life can change if you allow God's Word to speak to you!

So, let's talk about God for a minute. We know from your lesson there are three parts to God that existed in the beginning and still exist today. There is God the Father, the Spirit of God, and the Word, which later became Jesus Christ. Now, if you haven't done your study, then you might not understand this until you do the first lesson.

The Trinity was present at creation. Some people find it hard to comprehend the Trinity, but I like to use the illustration of water. Water can be found in three forms: a liquid (water), a solid (ice), and a gas (vapor). All three of these are water, but they all have different forms and purposes.

The Trinity also exists in three forms with three different purposes. God the Father is our heavenly Father. Jesus is God in the flesh, and He came to earth to die for our sins. The Spirit of God comes to live in those who genuinely believe that Jesus died for their sins. They are all God, but they have three different forms that serve three different purposes, and they were all present at creation.

God is also omnipotent, omniscient, and omnipresent. This means that God is all-powerful, all-knowing, and present everywhere all the time.

I find it very helpful to acknowledge these "omni" qualities when I pray. When I remind myself that God is all-powerful, all-knowing, and everywhere at all times, then I know that He has a full understanding and knowledge of everything I pray about.

In your lessons, you had some questions and verses about faith and prayer. It is important to understand the power of prayer. Prayer has to be based on God's will. If you don't read the Bible, then you are not going to know God and you will not understand His will. And let me say this—there is a difference between knowing scripture and applying it.

The Bible is a relationship book. It is actually a conversation between you and God. He communicates His will through His Word, the Bible.

Now, creation was believed to have happened anywhere from 10,000 to 4,000 years before Christ. Most scholars I have studied believe it to be more in the neighborhood of 4,000 BC.

In Genesis 1, there are several points to consider. First, God spoke, and things happened. In the course of six days, a vast expanse of nothing was transformed into day and night separated by the sky. Below it, the land, seas, and vegetation were created. Then the sun, moon, and stars were created.

Fish, fowl, livestock, wild animals, and creatures that crawl along the ground were created, too. And on the sixth day, God created a man and a woman to be the man's helper.

The second point in Genesis 1 is that God commanded the man and woman to be fruitful, increase in number, spread out over the earth, and rule over all the creatures of the earth.

The third point is God gave the man and woman every seed-bearing plant and every tree that has fruit with seed in it for food. He also gave all the animals every green plant for food.

Now, after I began writing the lesson that goes with this message, I learned some things I had never taken the time to think about before. First, God did not say the man and woman could eat the animals. Nor were the animals allowed to eat other animals. Every living, breathing creature on earth was only allowed to eat vegetation. This will get more interesting in future lessons when we study the fall of humankind.

At the time of creation, there was no death on earth. Therefore, everyone was on a vegetarian diet. It's not until Genesis 9 that animals could be used for food. Therefore, because death was not a part of life at that time, dinosaurs were in existence during the earliest human population.

It's interesting to know we were originally intended to be vegetarians! As a matter of fact, the book of Daniel highlights a story about Daniel's own dietary choices. He is invited to eat the king's rich diet of meat and wine but instead chooses a diet of vegetables and water. It ends up, after a period of ten days, Daniel looked healthier and more nourished than any of the king's men because of his vegetarian diet. Now folks, I am a meat and potatoes girl. I live in the heart of cattle country. However, this is worth pondering!

On another note, we cannot ignore the fact there was a morning and evening each and every day. In your lesson, I had you define evolution. This blows the theory of evolution out of the water because it is crystal clear that God created the heavens and the earth and every living creature over the course of a week.

God is all-knowing. He is omniscient. He knew humankind would come up with the theory of evolution. Therefore, He makes a point to create the entire universe in six twenty-four-hour days and inspired the writer to record it.

Some people will not accept God's Word as truth, and therefore will put their trust in theories. The fact is, if you are open to God's Word and desire to really know if it is true, then God will reveal Himself to you through his Word.

Having made the above points, I want to home in on one particular point. God commanded humankind to rule over the creatures and subdue the earth. In other words, people were to take care of the creatures and cultivate the land with responsibility. Not only that, but humankind is to respect the perfection of its design.

Friends, I always learn more than my students because writing a lesson or preparing a message requires me to do research and study many different resources to bring the fullness of God's Word to you! Now, I will warn you that I care nothing about being politically correct. If you have a complaint, take it up with God. This is the truth coming from God, not me. I am simply the messenger called to bring it into the open and point out its relevance in today's world.

There are two scriptures that correlate with God's perfect creation I want to talk about. He created the plants perfectly. He created the animals perfectly. And He created humankind perfectly.

The first scripture I want to reference is Leviticus 19:19. God commands this: "Keep my decrees. Do not mate different kinds of animals. Do not plant your field with two kinds of seed. Do not wear clothing woven of two kinds of materials."

Now, I have to tell you that my Bible study group freaked out because God said not to weave a cloth with two different fibers. It just so happens I majored in clothing and textiles. One of the first things we learned is you can't weave some fibers together because some fibers are stronger than others. This will break the weaker fibers. Therefore, you will end up with a weaker garment that will not hold up over time.

Another reason is some fibers must be cleaned differently than other fibers.

God's design is perfect, and Leviticus simply gives us care instructions for God's creation. So, no worries, ladies! You're not going to hell if you wear your favorite cotton and linen top today.

Technology has changed the way we spin our yarns and clean our clothing!

However, I do want to talk about mixing seeds of plants and crossbreeding animals. This warning especially got my attention when I began my research. In fact, I asked you to do your own research in your lesson!

First, let's talk about mating two different kinds of animals. In my research, I found that mating different kinds of animals could result in offspring that are often stillborn. This is because they have different genera and different numbers of chromosomes. An example would be a "geep." A "geep" is a hybrid animal that is a cross between a sheep and a goat. The sheep and goat are two different species. There are different kinds of sheep and there are different kinds of goats. What Leviticus is telling us is we should not crossbreed different kinds of species because they are designed differently. The sheep belong to the genus *Ovis* and have fifty-four chromosomes, while goats belong to the genus *Capra* and have sixty chromosomes. Even though sheep and goats are often pastured together, accidental hybrids are very rare. This indicates there is a genetic distance between two species. However, when humans force the hybrid union between different species, it conflicts with what Leviticus 19:19 teaches us about how to care for God's creation.

I would encourage you to do your own research concerning this matter. There are many questions unanswered, but it is important to keep God's creation the way He designed it and intended it. I personally don't believe we should be making "designer dogs"! If God wanted a labradoodle, He would have designed one! In fact, most hybrid animals are sterile. This is also of concern. It's just not wise to mess with Mother Nature!

Leviticus also warns us not to plant our fields with two kinds of seeds. Crossing two kinds of plants produces hybrid fruits and vegetables. This is done to get the best traits from each of the two plants into one plant. The danger is the seed often becomes sterile and won't reproduce true to the parent plant. This puts the original vegetable or fruit in danger of becoming extinct.

That brings me to the next topic: genetically modified organisms, better known as GMOs. Genetically modified foods are produced from organisms that have had changes introduced into their DNA using the methods of genetic engineering as opposed to traditional crossbreeding.

For example, genetically modified corn is designed to have a bacterial toxin (Bt) grow inside each corn kernel. This bacterial toxin is meant to attack the corn rootworm, which the corn is most vulnerable to. This worm attacks the roots of the corn plant, weakening and killing it.

GMO foods have been linked to toxic and allergic reactions. They also are linked to sick, sterile, and dead livestock and damage virtually every organ studied in lab animals. They're nasty things, folks! After I prepared the lesson on this, I went through my pantry and got rid of every GMO product I had. It is not natural to the plant or animal and therefore presents a danger not only to the plant or animal but the food chain that follows it.

The Institute for Responsible Technology reports sixty-five serious health risks associated with GMO crops. Nearly 300 experts agree that GMO crops are not proven safe, and they have significant restrictions or have been outright banned in more than thirty countries across the globe. So again, we should not mess with Mother Nature! Buy organic! Better yet, start your own coop garden in your neighborhood. At least you will know what you are eating.

On an entirely different note, and a politically incorrect one, I want to talk about God's creation and perfect design of males and females. There is a small explosion of transgender issues going on in our society. As I was preparing this study, I accidentally came across a verse in Deuteronomy 22:5 that I believe the Lord wanted me to see and talk about. Deuteronomy 22:5 tells us that "A woman must not wear men's clothing, nor a man wear women's clothing, for the Lord your God detests anyone who does this."

Friends, God does not make mistakes! He knew you before you were even in the womb. Psalm 139:13–16 says, "For you created my inmost being; you knit me together in my mother's womb. I praise you because I am fearfully and wonderfully made; your works are wonderful, I know that full well. My frame was not hidden from you when I was made in the secret place. When I was woven together in the depths of the earth, your eyes saw my unformed body. All the days ordained for me were written in your book before one of them came to be."

If you are struggling with gender identity, the Lord wants to help you! If you are a man, you were wonderfully made to be a man. If you are a woman, you were wonderfully made to be a woman. God designed you specifically as a male or a female for a purpose! The Lord does not confuse us. Satan does! If you are battling gender issues, your battle is not against what sex you want to be, your battle is a spiritual one!

In your lesson, Genesis 1:27 tells us "God created man in his own image, in the image of God he created him; male and female he created them."

It is crystal clear that God created you to be exactly what you were born as. God is a relational being. He sees, He hears, He touches, He weeps, He speaks, and He even smells! The scriptures that prove that were in a lesson you just did. God is there for you, my friend. If you reach out and ask Him to help you, it would be so much easier than changing your sexual identity. The Lord will bless you and He will help you correct your confusion, but He will not bless you if you go against His will as stated in Deuteronomy 22:5.

Every one of us has a struggle and we need to cry out to the Lord when that struggle seems like it is overtaking us. Our all-powerful, all-knowing, ever-present Lord already knows what your struggle is. He is waiting for you to call to Him for help because He wants a relationship with *you*!

God's creation was and still is perfect. He does not make mistakes, and nothing is impossible for God. He can get your mind and body in sync with each other if you will allow Him to help you with it!

In my Bible study group, we have prayed hard for two transgender people. After much prayer, both people returned back to their birth gender.

Satan opposes God. He is God's adversary. God commands us to multiply. We cannot multiply when we are confused about our gender, or when we have an unnatural relationship with a person of the same sex. Think about it! It is a powerful deception that Satan causes! The Lord would never give a command in the Bible and then create you in a way that would contradict that command.

On a lighter note, one more important lesson we can learn from Genesis 1 is God's work ethic. As I was combing through the verses, I really noticed some valuable, practical things. We all have those overwhelming days when we have too much to do and not enough time. Let's take a look at how God tackles His to-do list!

First of all, He kept things simple. God focused on the darkness and the light the first day. He didn't try to tackle an overwhelming list of things He wanted to create. Of course, He's God and could certainly handle it. But each day of creation, He focused on just a few things.

Second, He finished whatever He was creating before He went on to the next thing on his creation to-do list.

God is a God of order, and so the order of how He created the universe made perfect, logical sense. He started with the most basic element, light. Then, He separated the darkness from the light with the sky. With this in place, He could add the land, seas, and vegetation. Then He added the sun, moon, and stars; after the proper environment was established, He created all living creatures. After all the creatures were created, He created a man to take care of them and a woman to be his helper. This was a logical way to accomplish creating the heavens and the earth!

I noticed something else. He evaluated His work each day and saw that it was good. This was necessary before He went on to the next project the following day. He saw that it was good, and He was done for the day!

God even delegated part of the work to Adam. He told Adam to name all the animals! This gave Adam ownership in his role as caretaker of the animals.

How often I should have delegated things to my children around the house. Instead, I wanted to be in control of the way things were done. I'm a perfectionist about how towels are folded or how the dishwasher is loaded. Unfortunately, when we fail to delegate, we cheat others of their sense of ownership.

But not the Lord! Can't you just hear it? God probably said, "Adam, I'm done! You can name all the animals. I'm taking the day off tomorrow!"

The question is, do you take a day of rest? If God can take a day of rest, so can we!

So, in a nutshell, this is what we learn from observing God's work ethic:

- Keep your to-do list simple and achievable each day.

- Evaluate what you do each day, and when you see that it is good, move on to something else the next day.

- Complete one project before tackling the next project.

- Make your to-do list in a logical order! Make your errand list in a logical order.

- Share the ownership in tasks and delegate things others can help you with.

- Last, don't forget to reward yourself with one day of rest and relaxation!

- Not only is God's creation perfect but His work ethic is perfect, as well!

So, friends, I hope you have found these first few lessons to be interesting and beneficial! Like I said at the beginning of the message, God's Word is a classic book of guidelines, warnings, care instructions, and encouragement. It is always applicable and never outdated because it is God's voice speaking to you through the printed words on a page.

So go about your week, browse through your pantry, evaluate your to-dos, and remember that God cares for you and does not make mistakes! Let his Word change the landscape of your life this week!

Lesson 8

Genesis 2:4–25: Your Personal Planner!

Read Genesis 2:4–25 and pray that God will speak to you through this lesson.

Answer the following questions:

Let's think about what the scenery may have been like at this time. Eden was a pretty large area. Four rivers flowed through it: the Pishon, the Gihon, the Euphrates, and the Tigris. The Pishon River ran through the land of Havilah (north of present-day Yemen).

The Gihon River is believed to have run through the area of Iraq and Iran. The Tigris and the Euphrates rivers flow from Turkey through Syria and Iraq and into the Persian Gulf. I can't tell you the exact location of Eden or its size, but I can tell you it was in the area of our present-day Middle Eastern countries.

The garden was in the eastern part of Eden. It was paradise and must have been a gardener's dream! A mist from the rivers kept the vegetation cool and moist. Can you imagine the colors and smells of this garden? It had beautiful gems such as gold, aromatic resin, and onyx. The colors were bright, the smells were fabulous, the birds were singing, and the climate was perfect!

1. Looking at verse 7, what was Adam's body made from, and what did God breathe into Adam? (See also Job 33:4.)

2. According to Genesis 2:8 and 2:15, where did God place Adam and for what purpose?

3. What does Acts 17:24–27 say about when and where you are living right now?

4. Do you believe God has placed you in an exact location for a particular purpose? If yes, explain if and how you are fulfilling that purpose.

5. According to Jeremiah 29:11, what does this verse specifically say are God's plans for you?

6. How do you go about making major decisions in your life regarding marriage, job choice, buying a house, financial planning, etc.? Answer honestly.

7. Does Jeremiah 29:11 challenge you to approach these decisions differently? Why? What do you have to gain from it when you get God involved?

8. What did you learn that was new to you, or what stood out to you in this lesson?

Lesson 9

Genesis 2:4–17: Choices and Consequences

Read Genesis 2:4–17 and pray that God will speak to you through this lesson.

Answer the following questions.

1. According to verse 9, list the two significant trees in the middle of the garden.

2. What were the different consequences for eating from them? (See verses 9 and 17.)

3. What tree did God forbid Adam to eat from?

4. What would he gain and what would he lose if he ate from this tree?

5. Why do you think God created the tree of knowledge of good and evil if He didn't want Adam to eat from it? What purpose did it really serve? (See also Deuteronomy 30:11–20 for helpful insight.)

The Word of God tells us that obedience brings blessing. This was true for Adam, as well as the Israelites in biblical days. It is still true for us today.

6. How do you think this scripture passage in Deuteronomy affects us as a nation? What is the warning?

Which side of this equation are we on as a nation, and why do you think this?

7. When have you needed to turn things around in your personal life to get back in God's good graces? What about now?

8. When has God given you a clear warning about something? What did you do, and why do you think you did it?

9. What did you learn that was new to you, or what stood out to you in this lesson?

Lesson 10

Genesis 2:18–25: Chiefs and Indians

Read Genesis 2:18–25 and pray that God will speak to you through this lesson.

Answer the following questions.

1. According to verse 18, God knew Adam needed a helper. Identify four reasons in verses 18–25 for Adam needing a helper. (Refer also to Genesis 1:27–28.)

2. According to Genesis 2:21–22, how did God create a helper?

3. What does I Corinthians 11:8–9 say about the creation of Adam and Eve?

Adam was created *for* God and Eve was created *for* Adam.

4. What do the following verses tell us about our roles as men and women and husbands and wives?

1 Corinthians 7:4–5:

1 Corinthians 11:3:

1 Timothy 2:11–13:

Proverbs 19:13–14:

Titus 2:2–5:

1 Peter 3:1–7:

Which of the above verses spoke to you the most?

5. Pay close attention to 1 Peter 3:1. In what two ways does a godly wife win over her unbelieving husband?

6. Can you think of a circumstance where a wife has pushed her husband further away from God because she nags at him about spiritual matters?

7. What changes do you personally need to make as a man or woman or as a husband or wife?

8. Thinking about the work environment, the political arena, and in church and at home, name some ways we suffer as a society when these roles become blurred.

9. What did you learn that was new to you, or what stood out to you in this lesson?

Lesson 11

Genesis 2:20–25: Between Husband and Wife

Read Genesis 2:20–25 and pray that God will speak to you through this lesson.

Answer the following questions.

1. What important things do these verses say about marriage?

Genesis 2:24:

Malachi 2:15–16:

Matthew 19:4–9:

2. What are the only two biblical reasons the following verses give for divorce?

Matthew 19:9:

1 Corinthians 7:15:

3. How has society's attitude about sexual relationships and marriage moved away from the seriousness of these scriptures?

4. Do you believe there is a perfect marriage out there?

If you are going through a difficult time, do you suppose it could be a time of testing your faith? Explain.

5. Do you believe your marriage may be suffering or had suffered because of reasons pointed out in the previous lesson's scripture references? Explain.

6. You can't control what another person does, but you can control your own actions and attitudes. What changes do you need to make so your relationships with the opposite sex are more in line with God's will?

The old saying, "Let go and let God" is true, but we have to do *our part* and let God handle the rest!

7. How does Romans 5:3–5 speak to you concerning a difficult relationship you might be in?

It takes years for two people's lives to meld into one. There is a lot of give and take and growing and maturing to be done in a relationship. There are five basic steps to producing a fine bottle of wine! You could say producing a great married life is very similar. First, you must harvest your mate. Second, you must go through a crushing and pressing process that gets all the unrealistic ideas of what marriage is out of your mind. Third, a fermentation occurs. You both change from being selfish individuals to being selfless mates. Fourth, you get a real clarity about what true marriage is and the benefits of a life partner, a true soulmate. And fifth, you age together! This process produces a fine marriage that has stood the test of time and is well worth the wait and work that it took to produce it.

8. What did you learn that was new to you, or what stood out to you in this lesson?

Lesson 12

Genesis 2:24: In-Law Interference

Read Genesis 2:24 and pray that God will speak to you through this lesson.

Answer the following questions.

1. What does Genesis 2:24 say about the roles of mothers-in-law and fathers-in-law in their offsprings' marriages?

2. If your marriage is suffering from in-law interference, what steps do you need to take to establish healthy boundaries for your marriage?

3. If you have children who are married, does verse 24 challenge you as a parent? If so, why? What changes do you need to make?

What concerns do you need to turn over to God and trust Him to work things out?

I like to remind myself that I can't worry and worship at the same time!

4. Considering Malachi 2:15–16, who might you need to be praying fervently for concerning this matter?

As I grow older and enter the stage of life when my daughters are marrying, I am now aware of my own struggle to accept that things are now different between myself and my adult children. Having recently reached this stage in life, I am now understanding how my own mother-in-law must have felt when I became the main woman in her son's life. It is wise as a young bride or groom to be sensitive to this change your in-laws and parents are going through. Likewise, it is important for the parents and in-laws to let the couple become *one.* It is easier to become joined as one when there isn't someone wedged in between!

5. What did you learn that was new to you, or what stood out to you in this lesson?

Lesson 13

Genesis 2:15–25: Nothing to Celebrate

Read Genesis 2:15–25 and pray that God will speak to you through this lesson.

Answer the following questions.

1. After reading Genesis 2:15–25, also read Hebrews 13:4. Do you believe that God's view has changed regarding sexual relationships and marriage? (Refer to James 1:16–17.) Why?

2. What does Leviticus 20:13 say about how God views homosexuality?

3. What does God command man and woman to do in Genesis 1:28?

4. Practically speaking, how does homosexuality and gender confusion (transgender) conflict with God's command in Genesis 1:28?

5. What specific influences might be a cause for society to not take these commands seriously?

I once heard someone say, "If Satan can get us to laugh at something, he can get us to accept it." You cannot turn on a TV show or a movie or even a commercial without seeing a transgender person, or a gay or lesbian couple, or a bisexual person. The influence is everywhere. Years ago, you might see this in a comedy or lighthearted sitcom. However, now it is something we widely accept as "normal." Why? Because Satan got us to laugh at it first, and then later it became more comfortable.

Satan is the author of confusion, and he is the adversary of God. If he can confuse humankind, he can stop humans from multiplying as God commanded us to do.

Next time you see someone "celebrate" someone who has just "come out," stop and pray that God will intervene and clear up their confusion! Speak truth in love because you might save their life!

Love without truth is cowardliness. Truth without love is cruel.

We all struggle with sin, and we all need to be prayed for by others when we are living apart from God's will. The disturbing thing to me is that we are encouraging the lifestyle that God finds detestable when we celebrate it!

I believe that the Word of God has been so watered down in our culture, and we have become so politically correct, that many are unaware of the consequences of this lifestyle.

We don't come to God when we are clean; we come to Him because we are dirty. God brings us to Jesus. Jesus is the cleansing agent that wipes away our sin. The Holy Spirit is our power to curtail these sinful temptations. We all have temptations, but when we come to Jesus and lay them at His feet, they don't control us anymore!

Speak truth in love, with concern and compassion. Speak God's Word to those who may not know. They may not accept it right away, but pray it will plant the seed in their heart and mind.

6. Read *carefully* Romans 1:18–32. What does this verse tell you about homosexuality? Be specific.

What verse stands out to you the most?

We must make knowing God's Word a priority in our lives, and we must apply it to our lives. We can't pick and choose what's comfortable.

7. Look at 2 Corinthians 7:10. What are the two different sorrows this verse mentions? Explain in your own words how they are different.

What results in godly sorrow versus worldly sorrow?

8. What does James 1:22–25 promise to those who apply God's Word?

9. On the following pages, read my message on lessons eight through thirteen and write down your thoughts. What spoke to you? What challenged you or gave you inspiration? Write it down.

A Message from the Author

When you were a kid, do you remember playing with stackable cups? We all probably remember those! Or maybe you have a set of those Russian dolls that look sort of like cups and they stack inside of each other. I believe they are called Matryoshka dolls. Anyway, I was thinking about how that illustrates the message of Genesis 2.

As toddlers, we were learning the order of things with toys like stackable cups. The cups wouldn't stack together unless you got them in the right order. It's interesting that right here in Genesis 2, God is teaching Adam the order of things regarding men and women and the order of things in a marriage.

The Garden of Eden was a special place that God had reserved for Adam. When God created Adam, He created him out of dust. Dust does not have any moisture to it. In Jeremiah 2:13, the prophet describes God as "the spring of living water." So, when God breathed life into the dust, the water of life combined with the dust formed Adam.

The rivers in this chapter are located in the general vicinity of the Middle Eastern countries of Iraq, Iran, and Yemen. Streams watered the garden because rain didn't exist at this time. It wasn't exactly the barren landscape we are familiar with in that area today. In fact, it was absolute perfection, from its botanical beauty to its perfect temperature and climate.

Verse 15 tells us that God placed Adam in the garden to work and care for it. One of my favorite verses comes from Acts 17:26 (NIV). It says, "From one man he made every nation of men, that they should inhabit the whole earth; and he determined the times set for them and the exact places where they should live."

From these scriptures, we can know that God places us exactly where we are for His divine purpose. God chose the exact location Adam was to live and Adam's purpose was to work the garden and care for it. Adam was created *for* God for *this* purpose.

Do you ever wonder why you are living where you are? Maybe you wonder about it because you've never prayed about your purpose for being there.

Maybe you don't like the town you are in or even the neighborhood or house you are in! But Genesis 2 and Acts 17 tell us that God places us exactly where He wants us, and we have a purpose for being there!

Now there were two trees God pointed out to Adam. One was the tree of life, and the other was the tree of the knowledge of good and evil. Adam could eat from any tree, including the tree of life; but he was not allowed to eat from the tree of the knowledge of good and evil. Eating from that tree would result in death. The point is, God told *Adam* this *before* He creates Eve. You can see for yourself in verses 16 and 17.

God gives Adam the job of naming all the animals, and then He decides Adam needs a helper. So, God creates a woman from Adam's rib. Adam was created from dust and the breath of God. Eve was created from Adam.

There are several reasons Adam needs a helper. First, God tells Adam it is not good for him to be alone. So, Eve was created for companionship.

It was God's will that humans be fruitful and increase in number. So, God created woman to be beneficial and populate the earth with man.

She was also to help Adam care for the garden and subdue the earth. Together, they would manage God's creation and work together doing it.

We know Eve was created to be Adam's helper, and 1 Corinthians 11:8–9 reminds us: "For man did not come from woman, but woman from man; neither was man created for woman, but woman for man." Sadly, this has become blurred in our society. God has an order to His creation. If He had wanted the woman to be in charge, He would have created her first.

Have you ever been in a situation where there were too many chiefs and not enough Indians? Do you get what I'm saying here? Things do not flow well in situations like this. Do you agree? This causes tension, and often, chaos!

Our society has forgotten God's order of things and the purposes for His creation. Women, we are the Indians, and the men are the chiefs! I realize this is an unpopular thing to say, but it is the truth!

Women were created for men, not the other way around.

Have you noticed there are fewer manly men in this world compared to decades ago? When women insist on ignoring their roles as the "helper" and put themselves in the role of "chief," we not only emasculate men, but they lose their confidence to lead us.

The definition of *emasculate* is to castrate, to deprive strength of vigor, to weaken.

The synonyms for this word are to debilitate, undermine, devitalize, and soften.

The adjective of this word means "Deprived of, or lacking strength or vigor, effeminate."

Ladies, I can't speak for you, but I don't want a world filled with effeminate men. That is exactly where we are headed.

Men, I encourage you to respect women and appreciate what they have to offer as a female counterpart. Women are usually thoughtful, sensitive, nurturing, and caring. They have tremendous skills that complement a man in the workplace. Men and women think differently, react differently, and come from different perspectives. They also have different skills. When these differences are respected and valued, men and women make a great team!

Right now, there is a Me Too movement. Women are coming out and blowing the whistle on sexual harassment and sexual assault in the workplace. There are men who use their authority and power abusively toward women to suppress and intimidate them.

Let's remember the first man was created for God, and woman was created for man. If this would become the order of things in our society, we wouldn't have men sexually assaulting women. Men would remember they were created for God, and therefore act in a way that would be pleasing to God. Furthermore, we wouldn't have women disrespecting the authority of a man. We would remember we are created to be man's helper. We don't help when we undermine their authority or question and criticize their leadership.

In one of your lessons, you had to look up several verses concerning the behavior and attitudes of a godly husband or wife. One of my favorite verses is Proverbs 19:13, which says "a quarrelsome wife is like a constant dripping."

Does anyone like to listen to a faucet that constantly drips? It's terribly annoying! I really try hard to remember this verse, but I have to admit I can be rather quarrelsome at times.

Another of my favorite verses is Proverbs 19:14, which says "a prudent wife is from the Lord."

The definition of *prudent* is "wise or judicious in practical affairs, discreet or circumspect, and sober and careful in providing for the future."

Ladies, we are to "help" our husbands by being good stewards of the money they provide. We are to be wise and judicious in handling the affairs of the home.

If we are running up credit cards, our houses are chaotic and messy, and we're eating out of a box every night, then we are not "helping" our husbands. A man needs to come home to a peaceful, orderly home. That is how we help our husbands!

This might be an unpopular statement for some women. However, I had a full-time job when I had my first child. I felt stretched in a million different directions. We thought we needed both incomes, but I was so tired and miserable that my husband finally caved and told me to quit my job. I promised him that I would take care of everything else if he would focus on providing for our family. I finally quit, and it hadn't been two weeks before he got offered a job for twice the salary he was currently making.

I made sure he came home to a nice meal and a house that was in order. I paid the bills, ran the errands, had the cars serviced, and did all the other things that needed to be done. Basically, all he had to think about was giving his job the best he had to give. Together, we have accomplished so much for our family and ourselves. I believe God was right there, blessing us all the way, because Jeff made a great chief, and I made a great Indian!

God designed a pecking order for men and women to follow. When we submit to that order, God blesses us abundantly!

After God creates a woman for Adam and brings her to him, God declares something all married people need to remember. Verse 24 tells us that for this reason a man will leave his father and mother and be united to his wife, and they will become one flesh. The man and woman were naked and felt no shame. At this time, there was no sin in the world, and everything was pure and good.

This is the purist you will ever see a marriage in the history of humankind. There is nothing here about body shaming. There is nothing dirty, imperfect, or embarrassing about their naked bodies. Sex had not been cheapened by pornography or the blatant casualness of sex in movies and TV shows. In fact, the intimacy between Adam and Eve was just that—intimate, private, and sacred as God had intended it. They had nothing to compare their intimacy to because all they knew was what the two of them shared. My, how we have lost that in our world today!

Another point about verse 24 is that a man is to leave his mother and father and the man and woman are to become one. This might be a good time to ask yourself if your marriage consists of three people or more. Is a parent or in-law into your personal marital business too much? Do you and your spouse determine what your plans will be for Thanksgiving or Christmas? Or do you find yourselves constantly manipulated by a parent or in-law? Cling to one another, and don't allow the parent or in-law to control things. That's the order God gave in verse 24.

It's important to respect and care about our parents' and in-laws' feelings. Families should love and support one another, celebrate with one another, and enjoy fellowship with one another. However, the couple should cling to each other, stand up for one another, and make decisions as a couple without the interference of in-laws and parents. If you don't do this, then you leave space for a wedge to form between you and your spouse.

On another note, 1 Peter 3:1–2 says, "Wives, in the same way be submissive to your husbands so that, if any of them do not believe the Word, they may be won over without words by the behavior of their wives, when they see the purity and reverence of your lives." Too many women have a problem with this verse. Many women see submissiveness as a weakness. Being a submissive wife does not require us to be doormats. A submissive wife simply understands that the ultimate decision maker and authority of the household is the husband. She can offer her wisdom without being a quarrelsome, nagging wife.

In fact, it takes more strength and self-control to be a submissive wife than an overbearing wife! Again, 1 Peter 3:1–2 promises hope that an unbelieving spouse will be won over by the example of a godly wife who understands her place in the pecking order.

So, let's think about those stacking cups again. Whether you are a man or a woman, a husband or a wife, get in line according to God's pecking order. There's a good chance things will start falling into place!

Lesson 14

Genesis 3:1–24: Satan's Limited Power

Read Genesis 3:1–24 and pray that God will speak to you through this lesson.

Answer the following questions.

You are about to learn something life changing! Every day you get out of bed, you are in a spiritual battle even though you might not be aware of it. Eve was also in a spiritual battle, and she was totally unaware of it.

I want you to answer a question for me. If you were going into battle, what would be the most helpful piece of information you could know about your enemy? You would have to know what your enemy looks like, right? You would want to know the enemy's strategy, what territory the enemy is after or operating in, and how your enemy operates in general. So basically, identifying your enemy is your first line of defense!

When people start a Bible study, they usually want to learn about God. However, it is also important to learn about His adversary, the devil. So, in this lesson, I hope you learn the goodness of God as well as the deception of the devil. This knowledge will help you make better decisions and avoid the common compromises the devil will try to get you to make.

1. After reading Genesis 3:1–24, what do you find hardest to believe in this scripture? Be completely honest.

2. What other time does scripture record an animal talking? (Refer to Numbers 22:21–34.)

We know these talking animals were literal events because Paul refers to the talking serpent in 2 Corinthians 11:3, and John refers to it in Revelation 12:9 and 20:2. Peter refers to the talking donkey in 2 Peter 2:16. Many times in scripture there are allegories, but these were historical events.

I think it's hard for most of us to wrap our minds around a talking animal. Even the most highly respected scholars don't have an explanation for everything. Maybe that is why Jesus tells the disciples in Matthew 18:3 to become like little children. Little children believe without questioning. That is the same trust in God's Word that we must have. When we get to heaven, we will get our questions answered!

In the meantime, let's talk about angels. In the beginning, we know that God created the heavens and the earth. God saw

His creation as very good. When the heavens were created, the angels were created also. Angels, supernatural beings without bodily form, are created. They are ministering spirits sent to serve those who will inherit salvation (Hebrews 1:14).

Angels are higher than humankind (Psalm 8:4–5). They know more than humans but are not omniscient, all-knowing (Matthew 24:36). They are stronger than humans but are not omnipotent, all-powerful (2 Thessalonians 1:7). Also, they are not omnipresent (Daniel 10:12–14). They cannot be everywhere at one time.

There are different ranks and gifts among angels. Among these ranks include the rank of cherubim and seraphim. The cherubim angels have to do with the holiness of God violated by sin. They are seen "guarding the presence of God" throughout scripture. The seraphim angels are used to eradicate unwholesome attitudes.

In Genesis 3, the serpent is taken over by an evil spirit. This evil spirit had been an angel, created by God, who lived in heaven and had the ranking of cherubim. This cherub angel was the highest-ranking angel in heaven as well as the most beautiful. He was called the "anointed cherub that covereth" (Ezekiel 28:14–15 KJV). However, his desire was to be higher than God and usurp God from His throne. Therefore, he and some of the other angels waged war with God in heaven and, of course, lost! These angels were cast out of heaven and sent down to earth (Luke 10:18; Revelation 12:9).

In this chapter, we see the battle between God and this fallen angel, Satan, continue here on earth. That is why it is so important to understand who Satan is. Because if you love God, Satan sees that as a threat! His desire is to steal, kill, and destroy anything that comes from God (John 10:10). We see this in Genesis 3. Eve has been placed in God's perfect garden, and Satan is right there waiting to snatch her blessing!

Satan is still causing problems here on earth today, but God's authority limits him. This fallen angel, Satan, is known by other names throughout scripture. Devil, Lucifer, and prince of this world are some names he goes by. He is also referred to as "that old serpent," adversary, accuser, slanderer, murderer, and the father of lies, etc.

The devil is deceptive, and he masquerades as an angel of light. But he is nothing but darkness. His help here on earth comes from the other angels who were cast out of heaven with him. They are known as demons. As far out as this may sound to you, it is very real. Evil is real, and this is where it originates. If you believe Genesis 3, then you are on your way to understanding why this world we live in is the way that it is. Like I said, it is just as important to understand what your enemy looks like as it is to understand our Creator who loves us beyond comprehension.

On a side note, remember I said angels were created beings without bodily form. God created them before the creation of the world. Though they are without bodily organism, they have been permitted to appear in human form throughout scripture (Genesis 19:1, 5, 15; Acts 1:10–11). Having said this, many people believe their loved ones who pass away become angels with wings. This is not true. Angels are created as separate beings. When believers go to heaven, they are not flying around with little wings attached to their backs. Just thought you might like to know that!

3. What does Job 1:1–12 tell you about who is ultimately in control of what happens in our lives?

How does this passage make you feel about God?

About Satan?

About a difficult situation you may be in?

About the purpose for why you might be going through it?

Now that you have choked down this awful news about the devil and his demons, you can take comfort in knowing that God is and always will be in control! I'm not going to ask you to read the book of Job, but Job lost everything except his life. However, through it all, Job never stopped

Janice Bobanis

confessing his trust in God. And as a result, God rewarded Job by abundantly blessing the second half of his life.

4. Can you reflect on a time when you know God might have allowed something unpleasant to test and prove your faith is genuine?

5. What did you learn that was new to you, or what stood out to you in this lesson?

Lesson 15

Genesis 3:1–6: Brain Fog!

Read Genesis 3:1–6 and pray that God will speak to you through this lesson.

Answer the following questions.

1. Comparing what God *commanded* in Genesis 2:16–17 with what the serpent *says* in Genesis 3:1, what two things is the serpent doing here in 3:1?

2. Look closely at Genesis 2:16–17 and Genesis 3:2–3. What started the slippery slope for Eve?

3. List about four or five things that are happening in Genesis 3:4–6.

4. Can you think of an example when a person's disobedience to a God-given commandment is justified?

5. According to James 1:13–15, what are the stages of disobedience to God's Word?

6. Give an example of a time when you were lured into something off-limits.

How did you get to that point? Explain.

7. How does Genesis 3:1 describe Satan?

8. What did you learn that was new to you, or what stood out to you in this lesson?

Lesson 16

Genesis 3:7–13: The Cover-Up

Read Genesis 3:7–13 and pray that God will speak to you through this lesson.

Answer the following questions.

1. In Genesis 3:7, what did Adam and Eve realize, what did they do, and what did they use?

2. In Genesis 3:8–9, where is the physical presence of God at this time on earth?

What were Adam and Eve doing in these verses?

What was God doing?

3. Can you identify a time when you knew you were a sinner, and God was looking for you? Explain.

4. What is God giving Adam and Eve the opportunity to do in Genesis 3:9–11?

5. Who are the two that Adam is really blaming in 3:12?

6. What does Proverbs 19:3 say about human nature?

7. Who does Eve blame in verse 13?

8. Is there something you need to confess that you have been blaming others for? Explain.

9. Have you ever felt like God was giving you the opportunity to be accountable about something you did, and you were hiding your part in it? Explain.

10. Why does God lovingly confront us about sin according to Isaiah 59:2?

Many people who sit in church every Sunday and even those who attend Bible studies call themselves Christians. However, there is a disconnect with many when it comes to their relationship with God. It is a disconnect because they do not see the Word of God as a relational book. It is the best way that God can speak to us on a personal level when we invest the time to get into it. Many are just "checking the box" of going through the motions that most Christians are familiar with doing.

Adam and Eve had sinned. God was confronting them about it. They thought they could hide it. But when they knew they were being confronted about it, they thought they could deflect their blame to someone else. But God knew their sin and knew that it would separate them from Him if they did not confess it. Isaiah 59:2 is clearly telling us that God wants us to confess our sins for our own benefit!

11. What did you learn that was new to you, or what stood out to you in this lesson?

Lesson 17

Genesis 3:14–15: Sin Brings Conflict

Read Genesis 3:14–15 and pray that God will speak to you through this lesson.

Answer the following questions.

1. What does Jeremiah 23:24 say to you?

2. Read Genesis 3:14–15. For the serpent, what were the consequences for tempting Eve?

3. According to John 8:42–47, who do the following offspring belong to in verse 15?

Believers belong to the_____.

Unbelievers belong to the _____.

4. How would you describe the conflict between these two offspring today in our world?

5. Who will crush the serpent's head (verse 15) according to Romans 16:20?

6. What did you learn that was new to you, or what stood out to you in this lesson?

Lesson 18

Genesis 3:16–19: The Consequences of Sin

Read Genesis 3:16–19 and pray that God will speak to you through this lesson.

Answer the following questions.

1. What were the consequences for Eve's disobedience in verse 16?

2. What do verses 17 through 19 say the consequences would be for Adam?

3. How does 2 Thessalonians 3:10 magnify the intensity of God's discipline for Adam and all humankind?

Adam and Eve stepped outside God's hedge of protection when they chose to eat from the tree God warned them about. When a child goes beyond the boundaries a parent sets, either trouble or danger usually occurs. As parents, we must make sure appropriate consequences follow a child's disobedience. Otherwise, the child never learns the lesson. Consequences are painful reminders to not repeat the mistake again.

4. Give an example in your own life where the consequences of your sin serve as a painful reminder.

5. What did you learn that was new to you, or what stood out to you in this lesson?

Lesson 19

Genesis 3:19–24: What Happens Next?

Read Genesis 3:19–24 and pray that God will speak to you through this lesson.

Answer the following questions.

1. Read Genesis 3:19 with Genesis 2:7 and Ecclesiastes 12:7. What does Ecclesiastes 12:7 say about our body and spirit?

2. In Genesis 3:21, what did God have to do to get the skin from an animal so He could make garments for Adam and Eve?

God promised that death would come into the world if Adam and Eve ate from the tree of the knowledge of good and evil. Not only were there going to be lifestyle consequences for Adam and Eve to pay, but also the whole world would have to pay with death. Slaughtering an animal to make the garment of skin God needed was the first death that Adam and Eve had ever seen. This must have been quite traumatic! After all, they had cared for and named these animals. But sin is ugly, and it affects the innocent as well as the guilty.

Our omniscient, all-knowing God knew that Adam and Eve would cave into Satan's tempting offer. And as most of us do, they tried to cover up their shameful nakedness with a temporary fix. The fig leaves would soon begin to wilt, and so God slaughtered an animal to provide a more suitable and permanent covering for their exposed bodies. This friends, is the beginning of the gospel message. We can never mess up so badly that God can't save us from our shame!

From this point on, a human would have to sacrifice an innocent animal to cover the shame of sin. When Jesus died on the cross, He was the final blood sacrifice for our sin. Sin is what separates us from God. It takes the shedding of blood before we are cleansed, forgiven, and restored.

Before Adam and Eve sinned, they lived, worked, walked, and talked in the physical presence of God. But once sin entered the world, they could not be in the physical presence of a holy God. Death and decay entered the world. Our planet, as well as our bodies, have been in a constant state of decay ever since.

3. Read Genesis 3:21–24. If eating from the tree of the knowledge of good and evil led to death, what would the tree of life lead to?

4. If Adam and Eve had been allowed to eat from the tree of life after the curses and consequences were given, how would this have affected us all?

5. Do you believe that banishing Adam and Eve from the garden was punishment or protection? Explain.

In a nutshell, life was perfect for Adam and Eve in the garden. There was no death, no disease, no decay, and no hostility between people or even animals. They had actual physical access to God in the garden every day. It was a peaceful, perfect, and blessed place until Satan came in the form of a serpent to deceive and destroy that blessing.

God banished them from the garden so they would not eat from the tree of life. If they ate from the tree of life, then they and we would have lived eternity in a world of imperfection, decay, disease, and hostility separated from the physical presence of God forever!

My friends, Satan wants to deceive you and destroy your world as well! So, I'm going to lay this out for you in simple steps.

God is good and everything God wants for you is good and perfect! Satan is busy in your life right now trying to deceive you and destroy that perfect will for your life. As he deceived Eve and got her to question God's will as well as His Word, we too will fall for the same lies and many more lies!

However, the better we understand God and the more we can recognize the deceptive ways of the devil, the better we are able to resist the consequences of sin.

Eve was deceived because she was foggy about what God commanded them to do and not to do. Adam sinned because he was following another person rather than God. Those of us who take to heart God's Word, His promises, and His gift of salvation and restoration will one day, once again, live in God's physical presence here on earth.

God knew Adam and Eve sinned. He searched for them in the garden to give them the chance to repent. He covered up their shame by sacrificing an animal and making a permanent solution to cover their naked bodies. From then on, Adam and Eve, as well as you and I, must live and eventually die in an imperfect world.

Friends, Jesus was the final sacrifice for our sin. His gift of salvation and restoration is free. God looked for Adam and Eve in the garden. If you have *un*confessed sin, then He is looking for you, too! Is He giving you the opportunity to come out of hiding and confess your sin? God knows our sin anyway, and wants to forgive us, cover our shame, and restore us as soon as we will allow Him to.

6. Can you share a time you know God sought you out, you confessed, and He restored your soul?

We are absolutely helpless to save ourselves without Jesus, no matter how good we think we are!

7. What did you learn that was new to you, or what stood out to you in this lesson?

Lesson 20

Genesis 3:21–24: Finding the Gate!

Read Genesis 3:21–24 and pray that God will speak to you through this lesson.

Answer the following questions.

Jesus gave John a glimpse into the future in the Book of Revelation. Someday, Jesus will return. After the rapture of believers, the great tribulation, and the thousand-year reign, the Lord will destroy Satan once and for all along with his demons. At that time, the earth will be restored back to its original state. Believers will have access to the tree of life, and we will eat from that tree and live for eternity in a sinless, perfect world! And yes, once again, we who have been saved will live in the physical presence of our Lord.

1. What does Revelation 22:12–16 say about who *will* enter the gates?

Who will *not* enter the gates?

2. What warning does Matthew 7:13–14 give us?

3. Who is the gatekeeper in John 10:7–10?

Who is the thief?

4. What do the following verses teach us about our role and the devil?

Ephesians 4:26–27:

Ephesians 6:10–12:

2 Timothy 2:22–26:

James 4:7–8:

1 Peter 5:8–9:

1 John 3:7–10 (This refers to a deliberate, ongoing sinful lifestyle.):

5. Read John 3:16–21. In your own words, describe the person who prefers to live in darkness.

Describe the person who has found the light and how they are different.

Which one are you?

6. Remembering that Jesus was the final blood sacrifice for all humanity's sin, can you identify the first moment when you saw your sin and knew that Jesus died to cover your shame? If so, explain.

If not, why do you think you are unable to pinpoint that moment?

So, as we leave this lesson, I hope that you better understand the spiritual battle that continues on earth today. I want you to look at your battles differently because your battles are not really against flesh and blood. Your battles are against an enemy who wants to steal not just your joy but also all the goodness the Lord wants to bring into your life. He wants to steal your marriage and family. He wants to steal your friendships. He wants to steal your job and dreams.

We often become so angry with others that we can't seem to reconcile our relationships. If you can remember that your battle is not with that person but with the devil who is trying to steal that relationship away from you, then you can look at the situation in a whole new light. You can pray that the confusion and deception the devil is causing will be rectified with God's help through prayer. It is most helpful to be in the Word so that scripture can speak to you and change your attitudes as well as teach you how to respond to a situation or person.

Just like in heaven, the Lord will win this spiritual battle on earth when He returns! That is a fact, and that is the hope that believers have. As we live this life on earth, our bodies will age and eventually die, but our spirit will go to be with the Lord. When the spiritual battle is won on earth, we will once again be reunited with a body suitable for eternity, live on earth, and walk in the physical presence of the Lord. No longer will our sin separate us from His physical presence. The earth will be restored as it was in the glorious Garden of Eden. What an exciting future believers can look forward to!

Jesus said, "I tell you the truth, whoever hears my word and believes Him who sent me has eternal life and will not be condemned; he has crossed over from death to life" (John 5:24).

7. On the following pages, read my message on lessons fourteen through twenty and write down your thoughts. What spoke to you? What challenged you or gave you inspiration? Write it down.

A Message from the Author

Over the last few days, I've seen a lot of news reports about homes being consumed by fire. In fact, my husband even had a dream last night about a house fire. I'm always praying for the perfect illustration to make my point, and so I figured this was a good one.

One news report showed a father escaping a raging fire with his family. In the news video, the father was just starting down a ladder from the second or third story of his home with toddler in hand. As flames licked close by, the man had no choice but to throw his toddler away from the flames and hope the fireman below would catch her. Such a narrow target. It was a gut-wrenching video to watch. However, the fireman did catch the toddler, and everyone was OK.

Well, I couldn't help myself from using this as an analogy for Genesis 3. First, it's important to know how to prevent a fire. It's important to guard yourself against Satan. It's important to understand the damage that results from a fire.

It's also important to understand the collateral damage of sin. And it's important to know who can save you from a fire. It's also important to know the Lord is there to save you from sin.

In lessons fourteen through twenty, Adam and Eve are enjoying their beautiful paradise. Not only is working there a pleasure, but they also get to live in the physical presence of God. There are no worries or concerns. There is no sickness or stress; there is no death. In fact, they don't even have to be concerned about wild animals. There was perfect harmony between nature, humans, and the animals.

As perfect as this place was, there was one looming problem. In the beginning, when God created the heavens and the earth, He created the angels. These angels are created as supernatural beings without bodily form. There was one angel who wanted to be like God. In fact, he rallied up some of the other angels to war against God. As a result, God cast this angel and these other angels down to earth. Satan, or the devil as sometimes he is called, is the angel who wanted to be like God. The other angels who were cast down with him are known as demons. They do *not* have bodily form, but they are evil spirits.

Folks, we are on a spiritual battlefield here on earth because the war between God and Satan has shifted from the heavens to this earth. As in most battles, territory is usually what the fight is over. If you can imagine your heart as territory, the battle to win it is between God and Satan. Therefore, Satan is busy at work trying to usurp God and win your heart!

So, how does Satan do this? We begin in Genesis 3 with Satan, who has entered the body of a snake and is talking to Eve. Now this sounds a little strange to most people, but twice in scripture, a spirit enters an animal in order to communicate with a human. In this case, the spirit of Satan takes over the serpent. In the other recorded case, the spirit of God takes over a donkey. Rare as it was for an animal to be taken over by a spirit, it did happen and was recorded as such. The spirit used the animal to communicate with a human.

So, in Genesis 3, Satan occupies the body of a serpent to communicate with Eve and try to confuse her. In fact, Satan is called the author of confusion because he masquerades as an angel of light. However, Satan is darkness, and he wants to steal your light!

Satan's first strategic move is to get Eve to doubt God's Word. You have to admit, it's hard to wrap your mind around a talking snake!

Satan begins to confuse Eve by asking Eve a question. He asks, "Did God really say you must not eat from any tree in the garden?" Satan twists and turns God's Word. God had said they could eat from any tree in the garden but the tree of the knowledge of good and evil. Yet, Satan purposely misquotes God's Word ever so slightly and changes the meaning completely!

Reading this story is like watching a boa constrictor slowly squeeze its victim to death! After confusing Eve, he appeals to her logic, her pride, and her desire for food. Appealing to her logic, Satan says, "You will not surely die!" After all, Eve was not at all familiar with death.

He appeals to her pride. "For God knows that when you eat of it your eyes will be opened and you will be like God, knowing good and evil."

At this point, Eve begins to justify eating the fruit. After all, it was good for food, and it was pleasing to the eye. What harm could be done if she gained wisdom, right?

This was all a part of Satan's battle plan! Get Eve to doubt God's Word. Twist God's Word enough to mean something it doesn't say. And finally, get her to justify ignoring what she heard from God.

So back to my little analogy! How do you prevent a house fire? Well, you have to know where your vulnerabilities are. Is there a log catcher in your fireplace? Is your electrical wiring in good condition? Do you have old space heaters or unattended candles sitting around? These are all things that cause house fires.

The number one prevention we have against Satan's schemes is to know God's Word well! The better we know it, the less we will doubt it. The more we study it, the less he can twist it. The more we experience it, the more we will trust it.

Being sharp on God's Word is our first defense. When we don't know the Bible, it's like entering a battlefield without a commander. We won't know where the boundaries are, and before we know it, we have crossed over into Satan's territory!

I can remember a time when Satan was attacking my marriage. We were juggling life with two young kids, a successful career, and all the other "busyness" life throws at you. A wedge was forming between the two of us. It wasn't anything we purposely put there, but it was a wedge that kept prying us further and further apart. This wedge was a wedge of busyness and distraction that kept us from spending time together as a couple.

Now, I'm sure if you are struggling in your marriage, this strikes a familiar chord with you. We survived this challenging time in our marriage because we hung on to one particular verse in the Bible. Malachi 2:16 says, "I hate divorce, says the Lord God of Israel."

We evaluated our vulnerabilities, we turned to the Word of God, and we held steadfast knowing that if God hated divorce, He was going to get us through it. We knew God hated divorce, and so that became our boundary! We stuck out the hard years *together*! That is fire prevention, folks. Satan wants to destroy your life!

If your marriage or anything else in your life seems to be going up in flames, God really is waiting to rescue you!

After Satan succeeds in tempting Eve, she offers some of the fruit to Adam. When they both had eaten the fruit, their eyes were opened just as Satan had promised. But, instead of gaining wisdom, they were filled with shame.

Satan is full of lies, and what he promises will never come true. He makes a bad choice look good and a good choice look bad.

Adam and Eve felt exposed in their nakedness and their innocence was lost. As most of us have, they tried to cover up their shame by their own feeble efforts. They used fig leaves to hide their naked bodies.

They were living in the physical presence of God on earth at the time. They heard God walking in the garden, and so they hid. But God was looking for them, and He called out to Adam.

Adam answers. He tells God he's afraid because he's naked and ashamed. However, God gives Adam a chance to confess. What does he do? He admits he ate the fruit, but he blames Eve for it. When Eve is confronted, she blames the serpent for it!

I have a funny story to tell that illustrates how ridiculous we look when we don't take ownership of our sin. When I was a young girl, I had a friend who lived next door. She was quite heavy, and her mother was always trying to get her to lose weight. I, on the other hand, was nicknamed "French fry" because I was so skinny! Needless to say, her mother had placed my friend on a strict diet.

One afternoon, we took off on our bikes and visited the local candy store. We each filled a small paper sack with candy and rode back to her house. I will never forget it!

Her mother was standing in the entry hall, hands on her hips, with a clearly frustrated look on her face. She asked if we had been to the candy store but we, of course, denied it. What we didn't know was the bottom of her sack had gotten wet and the candy was falling out on the floor. We were toast!

The fact is, God's Word is there to protect us. Because He is a loving God, He gives us a chance to come clean when we sin. Too many times we think He doesn't see our sin. Or maybe we think we can cover it up, and the shame will go away on its own. Well, neither is true. God is omniscient and omnipresent. He is all-knowing and ever present. So, when we try to hide what we have done, we look like my friend and me with wet holes in our sacks and all the forbidden candy falling out all over the floor!

Blaming someone else, or even blaming Satan, will never satisfy God. He knows we have sinned. He will come looking for us so He can confront us and give us a chance to confess. However, even when we come clean with God, there are still consequences to pay.

In verse 14, God says to the serpent, "Because you have done this." God begins to hand out the consequences to Satan, Adam, and to Eve. They would each suffer personally as well as spread that suffering to future generations. In fact, these consequences will last until the end of earth as we know it.

First, God curses Satan. Satan will be the lowest of all the created. There will be hostility and hatred between Satan and humankind. There will be hostility between Satan's offspring (the unbelievers) and God's offspring (believers and Jesus Christ). Finally, God tells Satan that Jesus Christ will crush him by conquering death on the cross.

To Eve, God says He will greatly increase a woman's pain during childbirth, and she will be subject to her husband.

God then addresses Adam. Adam's first mistake was he listened to his wife and followed her in sin. (As you recall, Adam was created for God, not woman. So, Adam's first sin was he listened to Eve, not God). For Adam and all men, work would be harder than it had ever been before. There would be more effort required before fruits could be yielded from one's labor.

It's interesting to note that consequences can come directly from God, as in this case, or they can be natural consequences.

For example, if we smoke like a train and drink ourselves to death, the consequences for that will show up in our health. The point is, there are always consequences to sin, whether directly from God or as a natural result.

In this case, we see Adam and Eve's painless, stress-free paradise transition into a place where hardship and pain would be present. Not only did this affect Adam and Eve, but it will affect every generation until the end of time. The consequences of sin not only affect the sinner but the innocent, as well. Furthermore, what may seem like a small sin can have major consequences that last a lifetime. However, no matter how bad we mess up, God is there to catch us when we fall!

After God gives the consequences, He goes a step further. The fig leaves Adam and Eve were wearing just weren't going to cut it. They would wilt and decay and eventually expose them again. So, God had to take an animal, kill it, and make a garment out of the skin.

Now, it's easy to float over this part without giving it a lot of thought. However, up until this point, there was no death in the world. Not even an animal had died. In fact, Adam and Eve had never witnessed death at all! When God killed the animal, it must have been horrific for Adam and Eve. Remember, they had named these animals and cared for them.

Why did an animal have to die? Well, sin affects the innocent as well as the guilty, and the Lord will never sugarcoat its ugliness! This was the first time for sin, the first time for shedding of blood, and the first time for death. From that point on, throughout the Old Testament, the believers sacrificed an animal to cover their shame. Then Jesus came. He was the promised savior, the Lamb of God. This was prophesied all through the Old Testament. He came as a final blood sacrifice. We are all sinners, and we all need the shedding of blood to cover our shame. If we don't accept Jesus's sacrifice on the cross, we might as well be sitting in a house engulfed in flames.

Adam and Eve sinned, God confronted, they confessed, He covered their shame, and now we see God protect them. God banished them from the garden out of mercy, not punishment. The tree of life was still in the garden and if they ate of it, they would have lived an eternal life in a sinful, broken world. As protection, God separated them from that tree.

People are concerned because they think our planet is declining before our eyes. You hear people talk about global warming, an increase in extreme weather conditions, and so on. Friend, our planet is supposed to be declining! When sin entered the world, the planet began to decay and die, and our human bodies began to decay and die with it. This was not God's perfect plan for us, but God was prepared for our disobedience.

You see, God allowed us to have free will, but He did not allow us to choose the consequences. The consequences for sin are real, and we are suffering from them right now. These consequences serve as reminders! If there were no consequences, we would be more apt to sin. So, the consequences discourage us from repeating sin.

When we sin, God confronts. When we confess, God covers our shame. And when we believe, God protects!

One day, the Lord will return! He will throw Satan into a lake of fire with all those who are His followers. Then the Lord will restore the earth back to its original state, just like it was in the Garden of Eden before the fall of humankind.

We will have access to the tree of life, and all humans who have been covered with the blood of Jesus Christ will once again live in the physical presence of the Lord God for eternity. You see, Satan's plan is to steal our eternal paradise. But God's plan is to restore it!

Where do you see yourself right now? Do you need to work on some fire prevention? Or do you feel engulfed in sin? As long as we live, sin will be a part of our lives. But when we jump into the saving arms of Jesus, we won't be controlled by it any longer. We will sin, but it will not be a controlling factor in our life because the spirit of God will control us, not the spirit of Satan.

Every person falls, but not every person makes contact with the Lord! Jesus says in Matthew 7:13–14, "Enter through the narrow gate. For wide is the gate and broad is the road that leads to destruction, and many enter through it. But small is the gate and narrow the road that leads to life, and only a few find it."

Lesson 21

Genesis 4: Superficial Worship

Read Genesis 4 and pray that God will speak to you through this lesson.

Answer the following questions.

The first thing that came to my mind as I was preparing this lesson was the term "superficial worship." As we read Genesis 4, we are made aware that God's view of Abel's sacrifice was very different from His view of Cain's. I don't know if you are like me, but I often see myself as one of the characters in these stories we are studying. Sometimes, I see myself as one of the more unflattering characters and sometimes I can identify with one of the more distinguished ones. In this case, I see myself as Cain *and* Abel. I am ashamed to admit that I was more like Cain in my twenties but now, God willing, I hope God sees me as more like Abel.

Often in these lessons, I will ask you to look up a definition. Please use a dictionary. This way, your definition is more precise than a definition in your own words.

1. Using a dictionary, define *superficial.*

2. Using a dictionary, define *worship.*

As we begin chapter 4, Eve first gives birth to Cain and later Abel. As they grow up, Cain becomes a farmer, and Abel becomes a shepherd. Sin had already entered the world through Adam and Eve. To understand the reason God viewed Cain and Abel's sacrifices so differently, it's important to remember what we learned in the last few lessons.

When Adam and Eve sinned by eating the forbidden fruit, it was necessary for an animal to die because God used the animal skin to cover their shame and nakedness. We know that from that point on, people had to sacrifice an animal for the forgiveness of sin and for their relationships to be reconciled back to God. Later, God sent His only son, Jesus Christ, to die on a cross for our sin. He was the final blood sacrifice.

"Once you were alienated from God and were enemies in your minds because of your evil behavior. But now he has reconciled you by Christ's physical body through death to present you holy in his sight, without blemish and free from accusation" (Colossians 1:21–22).

So, keeping this in mind, answer the following questions.

3. Looking at Exodus 13:2 and Exodus 13:11–13 with Genesis 4:3–5, can you identify two requirements that were present with Abel's sacrifice that were missing from Cain's sacrifice?

4. In your own opinion, why do you think it is important to God for us to give our best and first like Abel did, rather than what is convenient like Cain?

5. What do the following verses promise to those who put the Lord first?

Psalm 37:4:

Matthew 6:25–34:

6. What did you learn that was new to you, or what stood out to you in this lesson?

Lesson 22

Genesis 4: Attitude Matters!

Read Genesis 4 and pray that God will speak to you through this lesson.

Answer the following questions.

1. Using a dictionary, define *righteous*.

2. Look at Hebrews 11:4. Abel was commended as a righteous man because of his sacrifice. In present-day church life, worship, and Bible study, how would you describe a person who had an "Abel" attitude toward the Lord?

3. How would you describe a person who had a "Cain" attitude toward the Lord?

It's clear from verses 5–7 that the Lord knew Cain's devotion was superficial. Again, like He did with Adam and Eve, the

Lord confronted Cain. Cain seemed to only want to do the bare minimum. Like so many, he was only checking the box of ritualistic to-dos. However, our omniscient God knows our hearts and can't be fooled by superficial worship. When our worship is superficial, then there is really nothing happening in our hearts. Sin is not being dealt with. Therefore, the sin just begins to grow until sinful attitudes turn into sinful actions and the momentum continues.

4. Do you believe we have become too casual with God? Explain your answer.

5. In your opinion, what makes a person casual and irreverent to God?

6. What do you think causes a nation to become casual and irreverent to God?

7. What did you learn that was new to you, or what stood out to you in this lesson?

Lesson 23

Genesis 4: The Unrepentant Sinner

Read Genesis 4 and pray that God will speak to you through this lesson.

Answer the following questions.

1. After reviewing Genesis 4, read Romans 6:15–23. Why does God confront anyone about their sin?

What does He really want *for* us?

What does He want *from* us?

2. If you are a born-again believer, what did you think you would miss when you were in your old life, and how do you feel about that now?

3. Read verses 11–16 and list about four consequences Cain would suffer for killing Abel.

4. The land of Nod actually means "wandering." According to verse 16, what was the immediate consequence for Cain's unrepentant sin? (See also 2 Kings 17:18.)

5. Using a dictionary, define *wander.*

6. Can you remember a time you were wandering apart from God's presence? What was your life like, and how did you find your way to God's presence?

7. What did you learn that was new to you, or what stood out to you in this lesson?

Lesson 24

Genesis 4: Constant Wanderer

Read Genesis 4 and pray that God will speak to you through this lesson.

Answer the following questions.

1. What does Romans 2:5–11 say the righteous ones will receive?

What will the stubborn and unrepentant receive?

2. What does Romans 2:13 say is the key to being seen as righteous in God's eyes?

3. What do you think the consequences are when we elect officials who do not represent biblically based policies?

What does it say about our attitude toward God when we vote based on party rather than policy?

Cain is the prime example of "superficial worship." He heard God, but he did not listen to God! We can sit in church, we can do our Bible study, but none of it pleases the Lord unless we take it to heart, respond when He confronts us on our sin, and make the necessary changes to get in a right relationship with Him.

Abel's sacrifice was pleasing to the Lord because the Lord was Abel's top priority. He gave the best and first of his flock out of obedience. He also understood that the blood sacrifice would reconcile him back to God. By faith, Abel was considered righteous because he understood that giving the best would result in getting back even more. You simply cannot give more than God. Even though Abel was killed, he went on to a perfect, eternal life and will spend eternity in God's presence.

4. We've talked about Cain and Abel having different priorities. Where has God been removed as a priority in our nation?

5. In your own life, how do you think the Lord sees your attitude of worship? Do you put Him first on your to-do list, or do you fit Him in where it is convenient?

6. What practical changes do you need to make to move God to the top of your priority list?

7. What did you learn that was new to you, or what stood out to you in this lesson?

Lesson 25

Genesis 4: God's Unconditional Love

Read Genesis 4 and pray that God will speak to you through this lesson.

Answer the following questions.

In Genesis 4:13–16, we see Cain afraid of being killed because it was customary that one who shed innocent blood would suffer bloodshed himself (Numbers 35:19–21). However, God put a mark on Cain to protect him from this happening. Cain, however, still shows no repentance.

1. What does this tell you about God's unconditional love for Cain, and in what way does this challenge or encourage you?

2. Who in your life does not deserve God's protection because of their unrepentant heart?

Does this example of God change your attitude toward that person?

Why or why not?

If you were to follow God's example of unconditional love, how do you need to respond to them?

3. Look at the following verses. 2 Peter 3:9 speaks of the Lord's patience, while Revelation 16:15 speaks of the Lord's swiftness. How do you reconcile these two verses?

4. What thoughts do you have concerning the death penalty in our court system when you think about the previous verses in this lesson?

5. What did you learn that was new to you, or what stood out to you in this lesson?

Lesson 26

Genesis 4: Are You a Cain or an Abel?

Read Genesis 4 and pray that God will speak to you through this lesson.

Answer the following questions.

When Adam was 130 years old, he and Eve had a third son, Seth. After Seth, Genesis 5:4 tells us Adam and Eve had many more sons and daughters. After all, Adam lived to be 930 years old. Therefore, the world was populating itself beginning with the first children of Adam and Eve.

Cain married his sister and had children with her. This was necessary to populate the earth and safe because there were no mutant genes in the genetic system at this time. It was not considered a sin of incest at this time in history because God commanded Adam and Eve to increase in number and fill the earth. We will study more about the people in Adam and Eve's genealogy when we get further along in the lessons.

We've talked a lot about Cain, so I want to talk about Abel for a moment. Many times, people can become jealous of someone's spiritual gifts or even their relationship with the Lord. Abel was targeted because he had something special in his relationship with the Lord. Have you ever been a target because of your spiritual gifts or your relationship with the Lord? Persecution can be very tough, especially when it comes from within your own family as in Abel's case.

1. What does Romans 12:19–21 tell us about how we are to respond when we are suffering adversity?

2. What does Proverbs 25:21–22 promise to those who overcome evil with good?

3. Using a dictionary, look up the definition for *sanctimonious*.

4. Can you describe an experience where you have dealt with this sort of person? How did you respond, and what were the results of your response to it?

Watch out for sanctimonious people, because they will be the "Cains" in your life!

As I was growing up, my mother was always very interested in politics and what was going on in the world. She always told me that when you don't think things can get any worse, the pendulum begins to swing the other way.

5. After reading about a series of "wandering" children in verses 17–25, what happened in verse 26?

Part of the reason I felt compelled, or even called, to write this Bible study is because I believe the world is suffering from an extreme case of Bible illiteracy. Many people call themselves Christians. However, their worship is totally superficial because they are living a deliberate, disobedient life apart from the Word of God. It is our own individual responsibility to know what God's Word says. He will not be interested in our excuses on Judgment Day! This is serious, folks. I am concerned for individuals who are deceived into thinking they have their salvation. I am also concerned for the nation I live in. God's judgment comes upon the disobedient. Are we a disobedient people because we are superficial worshippers, knowing full well what the Word of God says but ignoring it's worth? Or are we so biblically illiterate that we don't know we are a disobedient people?

I want to leave you with one last thought. I was driving down the interstate the other day and was considering if these lessons were the right length. Will people commit to doing the lesson in its entirety? I know they need to be a reasonable length, but the Lord spoke this to me that day: "If you want to know what long is, then try hanging from a cross for the day." Folks, that struck a chord in me. I realized that giving an hour to do a Bible study lesson each week is not asking too much. We can never "out sacrifice" what Jesus did on the cross!

And furthermore, we should offer the first of our time as well as the best of our time to get it done.

And He will reward us. Amen.

6. On the following pages, read my message on lessons twenty-one through twenty-six and write down your thoughts. What spoke to you? What challenged you or gave you inspiration? Write it down.

A Message from the Author

My husband and I were introduced to the sport of fly fishing about twenty years ago. I especially love fishing in the rivers of New Mexico and Colorado. Even though we don't get to fly fish much anymore, I still have all the gear. One of my favorite pieces of gear is my pair of polarized sunglasses.

The polarization in the lenses helps me to see what's going on below the surface of the water. They are a must-have for any fisherman!

This brings me to a point. You could say the Lord is a fisherman. He is a fisher of men! He watches us, He pursues us, and He is patient with us. He gets in the river of life with us and throws His cast out to us, just hoping we'll take the bait. His omniscient power is like a powerful polarized pair of sunglasses. He can see below the surface of our hearts and minds. And even though He might not like what He sees, He keeps casting repeatedly, hoping He will get a bite so He can take us home with Him.

Those of us who get hooked are transported into His loving hands. There is no catch and release. Once we take the bait, we are His!

We began Genesis 4 with the birth of Cain and later, Abel. Cain becomes a farmer, and Abel becomes a shepherd. Now we know that sin had entered the world through their parents, Adam and Eve. Their sin had to be dealt with by the killing of an animal. The animal's death served two purposes. The skin from the animal covered their naked bodies and the shed blood symbolized the cleansing agent needed to wipe away the stain of their sin.

God is a Holy God, and one must be considered "clean" before one can approach God. This is the most important and uncompromising truth about gaining access to God. And this, unfortunately, was the truth that Cain rejected. This is the story of two brothers. One takes the bait and the other swims away.

"In the course of time, Cain brought some of the fruits of the soil as an offering to the Lord. But Abel brought fat portions from some of the first born of his flock. The Lord looked with favor on Abel and his offering but on Cain and his offering he did not look with favor. So Cain was very angry, and his face was downcast" (Genesis 4: 3, 5).

In your lesson, I asked you to define three words: *superficial*, *worship*, and *sanctimonious*.

Superficial is defined as:

1. Shallow; not profound or thorough

2. External or outward

3. Apparent rather than real

Worship is defined as:

1. Reverent honor or homage paid to God

2. Formal or ceremonious rendering of such honor and homage

And finally, sanctimonious is defined as:

Making a hypocritical show of religious devotion, piety, righteousness, etc.

So, if I said Cain is a superficial, sanctimonious worshipper, you might think my description was a little harsh, because he *did* make an offering to God.

But let's watch Cain as the story unfolds! Cain brings the Lord some of his fruits as an offering. But Abel brings fat portions from some of the firstborn of his flock.

There are two problems here. Cain doesn't appear to be making any sort of personal sacrifice. We know he brought fruits. Were they his best fruits? Were they his first fruits? Did he look after himself first and give the Lord what was left over?

There's a second problem with Cain's offering. It was inappropriate. The standard had been set with Adam and Eve. A blood sacrifice was necessary for the covering of shame and the forgiveness of sins. Without it, there was no access to God. So, the fruit was an inappropriate offering.

And then something else is revealed about Cain. He becomes angry with Abel when God favors Abel's offering and not his.

Here are two fundamental indications of a superficial worshipper. A superficial worshipper goes through the motions of worship yet doesn't connect with the depth and meaning of worship. Cain can't appreciate the gravity of the blood sacrifice. The cost of sin is death. The death of something without sin substituted for the person with sin. But we can't appreciate this unless we see ourselves as a sinner. Our sin has to be paid for or we suffer eternal death. In the Old Testament, it was an innocent animal. In the New Testament, it was Jesus Christ.

Cain compares himself to Abel rather than comparing himself to the standard God set for sacrificial offering. Cain's view was horizontal, not vertical. He was looking at Abel rather than God.

Many people have a false sense of security when it comes to their salvation because they compare themselves to other people rather than to God's Word. It is God's Word that brings conviction and a chance to repent. This conviction pinpoints our sin. Statistics show that 55 to 70 percent of people who claim to be Christians believe they are going to heaven for good works or for just being a good person.

Many so-called Christians are good people, but goodness doesn't get you into the gates of heaven; repentance and the blood of Christ do!

In verses 6 and 7, God confronts Cain about his anger and being downcast. Cain is jealous of Abel's relationship with the Lord and wants to eliminate his competition.

God knows Cain's attitude is combustible. Cain is at a fork in the road. He can accept God's way of doing things or continue down the path he is on. Verse 7 tells us that sin is crouching at Cain's door, desiring to have him.

In previous lessons, we talked about being in a spiritual battle here on earth. God and Satan are battling for the territory of our hearts. And there was certainly a battle going on for Cain's heart!

In verse 7, God is making Cain aware of this battle. Choose the Lord's way, and you will master sin. Otherwise, it will master you! But there is no response from Cain. The conversation ends here.

Have you ever heard the Lord confront you on a sinful attitude? Have you ever heard Him warn you that you are spiraling out of control toward something worse?

To ignore God and continue on the wrong path will result in consequences we won't want to endure. Cain's anger toward Abel was out of control. He couldn't master it without God's help. He lures Abel out to a field and murders him.

But God is still in the river with Cain, throwing His cast and hoping His hook will set with Cain! God has on His polarized sunglasses and knows where to find Cain. He confronts Cain about Abel's whereabouts.

Given a chance to come clean, Cain blows God off! Only this time, God pronounces a curse on Cain. His sin has cost him the ability to produce crops on his farm; he becomes a restless wanderer, and he will now live apart from God.

He was a lost soul with no direction in life. Sadly, that's what we become when we choose our own path—lost, restless, and unfulfilled.

Verse 13 and 14 indicate that Cain was not remorseful about his choices in life but rather the consequences they had brought. We never see Cain accept responsibility for his actions. We just see him playing the victim of the consequences God had punished him with.

It's staggering to comprehend God's mercy and grace to Cain in the next few verses. When a person was known for shedding the blood of an innocent human, it was open season to take his life. However, in God's mercy, He marked Cain safe from that possibility.

It's amazing that God cares so much for every soul. Even those who blow him off! We all have those people in our lives we know blow God off. We can find comfort that God still cares for them and can offer them safety even if He doesn't bless the path they are on.

Cain and the Lord had their last conversation. If Cain wouldn't do things God's way, and Cain wouldn't confess to murdering Abel, then out from the presence of the Lord Cain went. Cain was left to wonder in the land of Nod. So, God got out of the river, put up his fishing rod, and went to another part of the river!

Nod means "wandering." This is a place where all superficial worshipers end up. They may be in church every Sunday. They might be teaching a Sunday school class. However, their worship is outward, and their devotion is superficial, not real.

Superficial worshippers love the idea of being a Christian. They love the idea of serving. However, if sin is not recognized, a disconnection occurs between the person and the Lord.

Hebrews 9:22 says, "Without the shedding of blood, there is no forgiveness of sin." Without forgiveness, there is no access to God. God brings people to Jesus, and Jesus gives us access to God.

Now that we know what a superficial worshipper looks like, let's take a look at Abel. Verse 4 tells us that Abel brought fat portions from some of the first of his flocks.

I am very ashamed to admit this, but when I was in my twenties, I know I was a superficial worshipper.

If I went to church, I was merely going out of ritualistic obligation. For instance, I never missed Easter and sometimes even attended the Christmas Eve service because that's what you do as a "Christian girl." I did love my Sunday school class because I could see my friends.

My involvement in any church activity was totally outward because nothing was happening on the inside of my heart! In fact, I didn't want to change a thing about my life. My life was fun! I had a successful career, and everything was good, so I thought.

When the "financial giving" form was passed out during the church service, I didn't really worry about it much. In fact, I thought it would be nice to win the lottery or one of those Publishers Clearing House giveaways because then I could be a "giver"! Problem was, I didn't have a clue about sacrificial giving. I certainly didn't understand the sacrificial price Jesus paid on the cross. I was a bona fide superficial worshipper! No better than Cain himself. A lost soul all dressed up and sitting in a church pew.

But Abel—oh, Abel got it! Abel understood that a sacrifice wasn't a sacrifice unless it cost him something. So many times, we pay ourselves before we pay God. So many times, we spend time on ourselves, before we spend time with God. But Abel didn't give God the leftovers. He gave God the first and the best of what he worked hard to produce. He gave out of gratitude, he gave out of obedience, and he gave out of belief.

Cain was jealous of Abel's relationship. And he murdered Abel out of the same kind of jealousy that killed Jesus.

The Pharisees, in Jesus's day, were the Bible scholars and teachers of the law. But they were superficial worshippers who didn't know God. They knew scripture, but they didn't know God. Therefore, they didn't recognize Jesus. And when Jesus came along, Jesus had a following. People tend to follow authentic believers rather than superficial ones. So, Jesus was drawing attention away from the Pharisees, and they became jealous. So, these "religious leaders" crucified Jesus.

It was all part of God's plan to provide a final blood sacrifice for humankind. However, here is the interesting lesson that comes from it: just because someone is religious doesn't mean they are righteous!

I have experienced persecution by people I least expected it from. After my first experience, a friend gave me a book called *Crucified by Christians*. Throughout the book a question was constantly posed to the reader. "Who does the crucifying?" it would ask. Well, I have to say that I wasn't expecting the answer I got at the end of the book. However, the longer I live, the more the answer makes sense. The Lord allows the Christian to be crucified by so-called Christians. That is, the Lord allows a true worshipper to be crucified by the superficial worshipper.

I now believe this lesson was for two reasons. One, so I could identify with how Jesus felt when He was nailed to a cross by the very people He came to save. The other reason was to curb my naivete about those who call themselves Christians. I now understand there are superficial ones and authentic ones.

If we are to minister to the world, it is critical to understand that not all people who call themselves Christian are true believers.

A true worshipper knows the prize is much more valuable than the pain of the perils. Abel was this guy! He suffered at the hands of a jealous brother. And even though he died a physical death, he did not suffer eternal death. Instead, he gained the prize—eternal life in the presence of God.

We are all going to die someday. But what kind of legacy will each of us leave? Cain would not leave a legacy that had eternal significance, but he would go on to build the first city. Through his lineage would come the first polygamist, the beginning of music and musical instruments, and the crafting of tools.

Abel would leave a legacy of righteousness. Recorded hundreds of years later in the Hebrew faith hall of fame and remembered to this day. Abel was the first shepherd, the first man to sacrifice an animal, and the first martyr.

I hope the next time you stand in a river, or the next time you wear polarized sunglasses, you will remember the important truths of Genesis 4.

Jesus says in John 14:6, "I am the way and the truth and the life. No one comes to the Father except through me."

Jesus is the bait on the end of God's fishing pole. You are either nipping at the bait, safely in God's hands, or you are swimming away!

Lesson 27

Genesis 5:1–32: Prophesy Begins to Unfold

Read Genesis 5:1–32 and pray that God will speak to you through this lesson.

Answer the following questions.

I don't know about you, but I have never been too interested in genealogy. This lesson has been particularly hard for me to write because I would rather talk about how to apply God's Word to our lives. However, the genealogy of the Bible is very important. It serves as a documented historical record showing the genealogical lineage of Jesus Christ. This historical record also proves the fulfillment of prophesy.

We won't cover every person listed in the genealogical account of Genesis 5, but we will home in on a few. And guess what? You're off easy this lesson! It will be shorter than usual because writing this was like sucking blood from a turnip! However, despite my shortcomings, I hope that you will establish an understanding of prophesy and the early patriarchs prior to the flood.

The first man on the list is, of course, Adam. According to Genesis 1:27 and 5:1, Adam and Eve were created in the image of God. God is an immortal being. So, Adam and Eve were created to be immortal. However, we know from lesson three that Satan, in the form of a serpent, tempted Adam and Eve to eat from the tree that promised death.

Seems so clear now, doesn't it? The choice between eating from a tree that promises life versus a tree that promises death. However, that's what Satan does best. He makes the bad look good and the good look bad! He lures us into bad decisions with his subtle, cunning ways.

1. Write down the definition of *prophesy*.

2. Look at Genesis 2:17 with Genesis 5:5. What prophesy is fulfilled in Genesis 5:5?

3. In Genesis 5:3, in whose image and likeness was Seth made?

Because Adam and Eve ate from the tree that promised death, their bodies became mortal bodies! And, over time, humankind's image became marred by sin. Decay set in, not only on the environment, but also on the earthly bodies of humans and creatures. That is why Seth was created in Adam's likeness and image rather than God's.

Unfortunately, thanks to Eve, we now have the knowledge of good and evil! Back then, the earth was still fairly new, and the sinful nature was still in its early stages on earth. It took many years for the sin to snowball and the earth to show signs of decay. Therefore, humans lived much longer and were able to populate the earth as God commanded.

As we read the genealogy of the patriarchs, the life spans are quite impressive. Most of them lived 800 to 900-plus years. Every father in this genealogical record had the one son mentioned, as well as other sons and daughters.

It's clear that many, many people were born into the world over the course of these long lifespans.

We know that Adam and Eve had two sons to begin with, Cain and Abel. Cain killed Abel, as we learned in our previous lessons. It was 130 years before Adam and Eve conceived their third son, Seth. Possibly this interval of time was due to grieving the loss of Abel.

4. Look at Genesis 4:25. What exactly does Eve acknowledge God for doing?

We are in a spiritual battle every day, right? Do you remember me telling you that in a previous lesson? We are in a spiritual battle because the war between God and Satan is now taking place here on earth.

Abel was a true, genuine worshipper, and Cain was a superficial one. Satan used Cain's jealousy to motivate Cain to kill Abel. Why?

It is because Abel was a threat to Satan! In Genesis 4:25, Eve clearly acknowledges the Lord for giving her Seth in place of her dead son, Abel.

5. Look at the genealogical record of Jesus in Luke 3:23–38. (You only need to focus on verses 23 and 38) Who is listed in the genealogical line of Jesus Christ in verse 38?

Bam! There you have it. Seth! Seth was the seed from which Jesus Christ would come. Originally, it would have been Abel.

Satan used Cain to eliminate Abel because Abel was a threat to Satan. It all goes back to the curse God placed on Satan for tempting Eve.

Genesis 3:14–15 says, "So the Lord God said to the serpent, 'Because you have done this, Cursed are you above all the livestock and all the wild animals! You will crawl on your belly and you will eat dust all the days of your life. And I will put enmity (conflict) between you (Satan) and the woman (mankind), and between your offspring (unbelievers) and hers (believers); he (Jesus Christ) will crush your head (conquer death by is sacrifice on the cross), and you (Satan) will strike his heel (nail Jesus to a cross)."

I am not a fan of snakes. We have a place out in the country, and we have seen some snakes! My husband told me that a snake's head is his vulnerable spot. If you can whack his head, you can kill the snake!

The verse above is talking about crushing the head of the snake, Satan! It is an image of Christ defeating Satan. Christ was nailed to the cross (the serpent striking the heel) yet He was buried, rose from the dead, and is sitting at the right hand of God the Father in heaven. He defeated the death sentence that Satan wanted to put us under. Those who believe that Christ (the final blood sacrifice) died on the cross for our sin, was buried, and rose from the dead, will have eternal life. These people are a threat to Satan because we belong to God!

6. What did you learn that was new to you, or what stood out to you in this lesson?

Lesson 28

Genesis 5: The Stand-Out Guy

Read Genesis 5 and pray that God will speak to you through this lesson.

Answer the following questions.

Adam had a son, Seth. It would be from Seth's line that Jesus would come. Then, Seth had a son, Enosh. Enosh had a son, Kenan. Kenan had a son, Mahalalel. Mahalalel had a son, Jared. Jared had a son, Enoch. Now, Enoch was a stand-out guy!

1. What does Genesis 5:22 tell us about when Enoch's walk with God began?

I don't know about you, but I was headed south when I left home as a new college student. And I don't mean south as in geographical location. I mean spiritually south! It wasn't until I had my first child that I found my way back to church and sometime later, a Bible study. Thank goodness. Whew!

2. What do verses 22–24 tell us about Enoch? Be specific.

3. What other details do we find in Hebrews 11:5–6 that tell us about Enoch and his faith?

Enoch lived before the first judgment on earth, the Great Flood, which we will study in future lessons. However, Jude 14–16 tells us that Enoch prophesied way into the future about the Second Coming of Christ. This will be when Christ returns to bring judgment on all the ungodly.

4. What does Jude 14–16 reveal in Enoch's prophesy?

5. Taking everything into account about Enoch, what part of Enoch's story touches you or challenges you the most?

I love what William McDonald writes in his *Believer's Commentary* about Enoch. He says, "To walk with God is the business of a lifetime, and not just the performance of an hour."

It is very possible that God took Enoch up to heaven so he wouldn't suffer the imminent judgment of the Great Flood. (That lesson is coming up.)

Moving down the genealogical record, Enoch has a son, Methuselah. Methuselah lived 969 years, and he died the same year as the Great Flood. He was the longest-living human recorded in the Bible.

Methuselah had a son, Lamech.

(Note: Cain had a son, Enoch, and also a descendant named Lamech. These two people are not to be confused with Seth's line of descendants named Enoch and Lamech. Sometimes people were named after relatives; hence, the duplicate names.)

Lamech had a son, Noah.

In verse 29, Lamech named Noah and said, "He will comfort us in the labor and painful toil of our hands caused by the ground the Lord has cursed." It is believed by scholars that Lamech is prophesying about the coming of Christ through the line of Noah. Christ will someday return and put an end to the curse humanity and the earth are under. The new Jerusalem and the new earth will be reestablished in the end-times. Noah means "rest." The conflict on earth will be over and everything will be restored to its original condition as it was before the fall of humanity. And hence, there will be "rest" for all believers, animals, and the earth.

You might find it interesting to learn in future lessons that the very long life spans begin to shorten after the flood.

6. What does Psalm 90:10 say the average life expectancy was when Moses wrote this Psalm?

Noah had three sons, Shem, Ham, and Japheth. We will study about these three sons in a future lesson.

As we close, we can reflect on these men, their sons, and their lives. Seth would be the line from which Jesus Christ would come. Therefore, this line of descendants would be Satan's biggest threat in his war against God. In future lessons, I want you to think about the obstacles and adversity these descendants faced. I also want you to think about the perseverance these people had to have. Some were just ordinary, godly people. But others were standouts! Who were the standouts? Why did they stand out? What did they accomplish in life? And how did their accomplishments benefit humanity?

I challenge you to insert yourself into each and every story. How can you be a standout for the Lord? Are you content with being an ordinary godly person? Or is the Lord calling you to something bigger?

It was not until after Enoch became the father of Methuselah that he began to walk with God. Folks, it is never too late to do something remarkable with your life. I can so relate to Enoch! I didn't start going back to church until I had my first child, just like Enoch. I got into a Bible study and was saved while studying the book of John. At that point,

God called me into ministry. I received my spiritual gift of teaching. And here I am, hoping to change the world by writing a Bible study.

7. Is the Lord calling you? If you know He is, then what are you waiting for? Can you share this with others and maybe share what is causing you to hesitate?

Jesus tells His disciples in Matthew 9:37–38, "The harvest is plentiful but the workers are few. Ask the Lord of the harvest, therefore, to send out workers into his harvest field."

Maybe your harvest is your family or among your friends. But to be a standout follower is making your walk with God your lifetime business!

8. On the following pages, read my message on lessons 27 and 28. Write down your thoughts. What spoke to you? What challenged you or gave you inspiration? Write it down.

A Message from the Author

I find it so comforting that humankind cannot thwart God's plan. God planned for us to live in His physical presence here on earth. A life free of sickness, strife, and death. Even though Adam and Eve disrupted that plan, they only disrupted it for a set time. Today, we are going to review the genealogy from Adam to Noah. We will look at how God protects His plan for humankind through this genealogy.

To begin, I want you to picture a big bowl of jelly beans. If you are familiar with jelly beans, then you know there is one noticeable jelly bean that stands out among the others. It's the black jelly bean with the licorice taste. Some people love them, and others avoid them.

That's what I think about when I think of the genealogy of Adam to Noah. There is a line of descendants coming from Adam but only a few are standouts. These standouts were people who made God their business of a lifetime rather than just a business of an hour. I'm sure you understand what I'm talking about. Some people think about the Lord on Sunday morning, while others make Him a priority throughout the week.

If you are particularly focused and make the Lord known in all areas of your life, then you are probably like the black jelly bean! Some people are drawn to you while others avoid you.

Early in biblical history, Adam and Eve were doing their part fulfilling the command to multiply and fill the earth. We know they had Cain and Abel, as well as other sons and daughters. The records in Genesis 4 tell us the population was growing on earth. The marriages between siblings and relatives were the only means of procreation at that time. Not until Moses's time were these relations considered sinful. The population had become large enough that procreation among close relatives was no longer necessary. In fact, Leviticus 18 describes laws forbidding sexual relations between close relatives.

So that brings us to the genealogy of Adam to Noah. We know from previous lessons the spiritual battle between God and Satan is taking place on earth. Satan tempted Eve, she believed the lie, and sin and death came into the world.

We know from Genesis 3:15 that God placed a curse on Satan. God says to Satan, "I will put enmity between you and the woman, and between your offspring and hers; he will crush your head, and you will strike his heel."

This verse describes the conflict between believers and nonbelievers, and the conflict between Satan and Christ. In this verse, Satan will strike at Jesus, but Jesus will conquer Satan's death wish for humankind by His sacrificial death on the cross.

With this curse, comes a fight! Satan is determined to sever the genealogical line from which Jesus would come.

Therefore, Satan uses Cain to kill Abel! Why? Because Jesus would have come from the lineage of Abel.

When Adam was 130 years old, long after the death of Abel, Adam and Eve give birth to Seth. In Luke 3:38, we find Seth to be an ancestor of Jesus. So, our omnipotent God continues the line from which Jesus would come despite Satan's attempts to sever it.

After Seth was born, Adam lived 800 more years, giving Adam a lifespan of 930 years. Seth had a son, Enosh. Enosh had a son, Kenan. Kenan had a son, Mahalalel. Mahalalel had a son, Jared. Jared had a son, Enoch.

The verses describing this genealogy tell us that all these fathers had many other sons and daughters. The fathers lived anywhere from 800 to 900-plus years. Now all these people mentioned previously were regular old jelly beans! But the last name I mentioned, Enoch, well, he was special. He stood out!

Genesis 5:21–22 tell us that Enoch had a son, Methuselah. And it wasn't until Methuselah was born that Enoch began to walk with God. Now, just for the record, I can really relate to this guy, Enoch. I too was just a regular old jelly bean until by first daughter was born. For many of us, we think because we have a child, we need to get back to church for the child's sake. Little did I know that I needed to get back to church for *my* sake!

Well, apparently, ol' Enoch decided it was time for him to do the same! He didn't have a relationship with God until his child was born. After the birth of Methuselah, Enoch walked with God for 300 years, and then he was no more because God took him away.

There is only one other person mentioned in the Bible that God "took away." In other words, they did not experience a physical death. That person was Elijah. 2 Kings 2:1 tells us God took Elijah up to heaven in a whirlwind. Both men were "taken away" by God. This is a glimpse of the rapture when Jesus comes for the believers before the Great Tribulation. We will be "taken up" to heaven along with the believers who have previously died.

Enoch walked with God for 300 years. So, what does it mean to "walk" with God? Well, William McDonald says it best in his *Believer's Commentary*: "To walk with God is the business of a lifetime, and not just a performance of an hour."

Enoch made God his lifetime business and that's what separates the regular jelly beans from the standout! Enoch's spiritual gift was prophecy. You can find his prophetic message in the book of Jude verses 14–16. He prophesied about the Second Coming of Christ and the judgment that will come to all the godless people. He was the jelly bean that people either listened to or avoided. He told the truth and sometimes the truth is hard to swallow!

When Enoch's son, Methuselah, lived 187 years, he became the father of Lamech. Later, Lamech would become the father of Noah.

Methuselah was the oldest recorded human in history; living 969 years and dying the year of the flood. And for his last 120 years, he would watch his grandson, Noah, prepare for that flood.

Noah, another noticeable jelly bean, was specifically called by God to build an ark. No one had ever seen rain or even knew what rain was, *including* Noah! Nevertheless, Noah did not doubt God! In fact, no one other than Noah and his family believed God would send judgment on the earth.

It would take Noah 120 years to build something that the entire world thought was foolish. But a person who makes the Lord their lifetime business knows God's business.

In fact, Jesus tells His disciples in John 15:15, "I no longer call you servants, because a servant does not know his master's business. Instead, I have called you friends, for everything that I learned from my Father I have made known to you."

The black jelly beans are the stand-out jelly beans in a bowl full of regular jelly beans. And in this world, they know God's business. Enoch knew God's business and prophesied the Second Coming of Christ. Noah knew God's business and he prepared for a catastrophic flood that God warned him about.

Abel, Enoch, and Noah were the black jelly beans of their day. They were the ones making a difference. Hebrews 11 is an account of those throughout biblical history whose faith was put to the extreme test. And yet, they persevered through it all. It is called the Hebrew Faith Hall of Fame.

Would you expect anything less from the ancestors of Jesus Christ? It takes this kind of faith when you are on the front lines of the spiritual conflict between God and Satan. Satan doesn't want you to know *about* God's judgment, and he certainly doesn't want you to *fear* it!

History proves that those who ignore the warnings of judgment will die at the hands of it. So, God doesn't use the ordinary old jelly beans to do His fighting. He uses the ones who make God their lifetime business.

After Noah was 500 years old, he became the father of Shem, Ham, and Japheth. A few lessons from now, we will study about the flood. We will witness Noah, his three sons, and their wives survive the flood as well as the aftermath.

After the flood, God commanded Noah and his family to multiply and fill the earth. We will see Noah's descendants settle in Babel against God's will. Because of their disobedience, God confused their language and scattered them across the world. From this scattering, different nations and different languages developed. Shem, however, would be the only genealogical line from Noah's family to maintain the Hebrew language. Furthermore, it would be Shem's lineage from which Jesus would come.

So, there are two important truths I want you to walk away with today.

First, nothing thwarts God's plan for humankind. God's plan was to walk among us on earth and have fellowship with us as He did with Adam and Eve. However, Satan tried to put a death sentence on humankind by getting Eve to eat from the tree that promised death. Now we suffer a physical death and physical separation from God.

However, God cannot be thwarted. Through the genealogical line of Seth, Enoch, Noah and Shem, the birth of Jesus would come. He would crush Satan by conquering death on the cross, substituting Himself as a blood sacrifice and giving us eternal life.

"For God so loved the world that he gave his one and only Son, that whoever believes in him shall not perish but have eternal life" (John 3:16).

In Revelation, Jesus reveals to John that He will return some day. Jesus will judge the unbelievers and do away with Satan forever. The conflict between God and Satan will end. The conflict between believers and unbelievers will end. Earth will be restored back to its original perfection as it was in the Garden of Eden. Furthermore, we will once again walk in the physical presence of God as Adam and Eve did before sin entered the world.

God's plan cannot be thwarted. He never allowed Satan to permanently sever the genealogical lineage that led to the birth of Jesus Christ.

That's the first point I want you to walk away with today. The second point is this: The Lord needs people who stand out in a crowd. Are you just an ordinary jelly bean, or is God calling you to be more than that?

Ordinary jelly beans are still jelly beans, but those who stand out make the most difference. I can remember when all the dots connected for me when I was thirty-two. I came to a genuine belief in Jesus Christ. I received the Holy Spirit, and I also received my spiritual gift. Although I didn't know I had received my spiritual gift of teaching, God began preparing me to use it in the future.

A man once told me, "God doesn't call the prepared; he prepares the called." This is very true.

Shortly after I became a true believer, I attended a meeting at the church I belonged to. They needed a vacation Bible school director. Well, strangely enough, my hand rose in the air and seemed to supernaturally volunteer for the job!

As I got involved in the process, I realized this vacation Bible school had little to do with the Bible and a lot to do with crafts! I became very passionate about teaching these children *and* the VBS teachers the importance of making God's Word the central focus of VBS.

This experience was the beginning of God's preparation of me to become a teacher of His Word. I never in a million years ever thought I would be where I am today. And so, that leads me to another point.

There are two different kinds of calling. The Lord may call us to do something generally, *or* He may call us to do something specific.

When I was at the church meeting, He was calling me generally. The church needed a VBS director, and I volunteered. It was equal to the experience of Isaiah 6:8. The Lord is looking for a volunteer.

Isaiah says, "Then I heard the voice of the Lord saying, "Whom shall I send? And who will go for us?" and I said, "Here am I. Send me!"

That is God's "general" calling.

Then there is God's specific calling. And I mean *specific*! This occurs when He has *you* in mind for the job!

When I was in my very early forties, I had several years of serving the Lord under my belt. I had directed VBS and written the VBS curriculum two years in a row. I was also a children's teacher in a large international Bible study. Then I wrote a short, two-semester Bible study for my neighborhood and led that.

Then came the *specific* call. The one there is no mistake about!

At the time of this call, I was frustrated with the constraints of writing an entire curriculum on paper. I felt I couldn't get my heart expressed with paper and ink. Many of the neighbors were calling about the next study, but I hadn't started it yet due to my frustration.

To make a long story very short, I was ironing one day and praying about the situation. I put the iron down and went to my closet where I really pray! God called me specifically while I was on my knees in prayer in the privacy of my closet! His words were almost audible. He said to me, "Your fear of speaking in front of people is in the way of what I have for you!"

Well, I have to say that no one knows your weakness better than the Lord. He nailed me! I was terrified of speaking even to the smallest Sunday school class. I'm telling you that I wouldn't and couldn't make myself give a class announcement or prayer request!

Anyway, within a year, I found myself behind a podium teaching one hundred-plus women in a Bible study. God called me where I was *least comfortable yet most prepared!*

We know Noah was specifically called to build the ark. Moses is a great example, as well. God specifically called Moses to lead the Israelites out of Egyptian slavery. God did this not in Moses's walk-in closet, but through a burning bush in a pasture!

Moses, like me, had a weakness. He stuttered! He even asked God if Aaron could speak for him. This angered God because God often calls us where we have weakness so we will depend on Him through the process. He wants to be our crutch, not other people!

God had prepared Moses for this calling. Moses had grown up in the pharaoh's house. He had firsthand knowledge of their military strategies and other helpful insights.

So, friend, there you have it! God calls us generally and specifically to make a difference in the world. Make God your lifetime business and He will take you on an adventure of a lifetime! It is the closest thing to walking in the physical presence of God Himself.

Remember, nothing and no one can thwart God's plan for you! He can take a regular ol' jelly bean and turn you into one that stands out. However, you must trust Him with your weakness and believe that He has prepared you for the call.

Lesson 29

Genesis 6: Flood Warning, Part One

Read Genesis 6 and pray that God will speak to you through this lesson.

Answer the following questions.

As I took a helicopter view of this chapter, I divided it into three parts. First, I saw God filled with pain as He looked upon the earth and saw all the evil. Second, I saw God warn Noah about what He would do about it. Third, I saw God give Noah instruction on how to plan for it.

What came to my mind was a quote my husband once said to me. Being in the financial business, his philosophy was, "The higher the risk, the greater the return on your investment!" Now, I know this can be true in the stock market. It's also true when we risk what others think of us and obey God even though it doesn't make sense at the time.

It's obvious from the early verses of Genesis 6 that evil and immorality had flourished among the populated earth.

However, these verses are very hard to understand, even among scholars. I have researched and studied these verses quite a bit, and I'm sorry to say there are no concrete answers as to exactly who the "sons of God" and "the daughters of men" are.

Some theorize the "sons of God" are the fallen angels who married the "daughters" of mortal humans. This theory is mentioned in most commentaries but not totally accepted for various reasons. The other idea is the "sons of God" are from the line of Seth (representing believers) and the "daughters of men" are from the line of Cain (representing unbelievers).

When you jump down to verse 4, the Nephilim are mentioned. The Hebrew word for Nephilim is *Naphal*, meaning "fall." This name could refer to "fallen ones," which takes us back to the theory of "sons of God" being the fallen angels cast out of heaven with Satan. These cast-down angels can appear in human form, but it is questionable if they can have children. That is why this theory is a little shaky!

So, as you can see, there are many unanswered questions about exactly whom these two groups are referring to. We do know believers and unbelievers were unevenly yoked, diluting a pure devotion to God. Hence, this resulted in a downward spiral of morality into the depths of a corrupt and evil world. Therefore, the Lord had to put an end to it and the "end" would come in exactly 120 years!

1. What does Genesis 1:31 say about how God felt the week of creation?

2. What do Genesis 6:6 and 1 Samuel 15:11 have in common?

3. Describe a time when you did something good for someone, and they betrayed you later. How did that make you feel? Did it change your relationship with that person? Explain.

It's a sobering thought, but I know I've been blessed by God, yet I've disappointed Him on occasion.

4. What was special about each person's relationship with the Lord in the following verses?

Moses in Exodus 33:11:

Moses in Exodus 33:17:

The disciples with Jesus in John 15:15:

Abraham in James 2:23:

In my young adult years, I had a lot of friends, but I didn't have that one special friend I could confide in. I later learned how to make those kinds of friends by observing my husband. One day, he told me straight out that I didn't have any close friends because I didn't invest the time in anyone. Wow! He was so right!

Friendship is work! It takes time to develop a relationship by listening, communicating, and making what's important to them important to you. This is also, ironically, how I made friends with the Lord. I have to say, He is my best friend! He knows me better than anyone else. I trust Him, and I know He will tell me what I need to hear, not what I want to hear. I can talk to Him anytime I want! He is always available. In fact, I spend more time with the Lord than anyone else!

It really doesn't matter what your environment is, you can still have a strong, dynamic relationship with the Lord. Look at Noah. He was living in a totally corrupt world surrounded by ungodly influences. Yet, Noah could still hear God because he was so familiar with His voice! This is not an audible voice, but when you hear God speak to you, you will know it! I can't describe it really, but it is just something you experience when you have a deep personal relationship with Him. It's not constant, and maybe that is why I recognize it. It is unlike anything else.

5. Can you describe a time when you knew you heard the Lord speak to you so clearly there was no doubt you were hearing the Lord? Did you obey? How did things transpire after that?

If you don't feel you have ever heard the Lord speak to you, what can you do better to invest in that friendship?

6. What did you learn that was new to you, or what stood out to you in this lesson?

Lesson 30

Genesis 6: Flood Warning, Part Two

Read Genesis 6 and pray that God will speak to you through this lesson.

Answer the following questions.

1. What do verses 8 and 9 tell us about Noah?

2. What do verses 11–13 say about what the world was like at this time?

You talk about a tough environment! Remaining in God's favor must have been quite a challenge for Noah. He was bombarded with worldly pressures in that day and time. Yet, God chose to reveal a most important decision to Noah concerning the imminent judgment upon the earth. The Lord considered Noah a friend more than a servant. Therefore, God was revealing His plan of judgment to Noah with specific instructions on how to prepare for it.

To put things into perspective at that time, Henry M. Morris writes in *Genesis Record* that he believes there were 1,656 years from the time of creation to the time of the flood (assuming there are no time gaps in the genealogies). If you take the recorded genealogical record at face value, then Adam lived until Lamech (the father of Noah) was fifty-six years old. Noah was born only fourteen years after the death of Seth. These men were the primary ones responsible for ministering God's Word to the people. However, from the looks of things, the ministry of God's Word fell on deaf ears!

You know, women go to lunch and men go to breakfast. I know you know what I'm talking about. When my Bible study ladies and I go to lunch, we start talking about world events. Can't you just see it? I wonder if these patriarchs had a standing breakfast date each morning! I bet they talked about how the world was going to hell in a handbasket. You know, like we do! In fact, that was my mother's favorite saying. As she watched the evening news, she would shake her head and say, "Oh, for heaven's sake! Our world is just goin' ta hell in a handbasket!"

I'm making a lighthearted point about something very serious. Judgment is real. History and scientific data prove that. A nation that has turned its back on God will face certain judgment if it refuses to turn back to Him.

I live in the United States of America, and we have passed laws that totally contradict the Word of God. We have passed laws that support gay marriage and abortion rights and late-term abortions. We are currently struggling with transgender rights. Transgender people want to use the bathroom of their gender "identity" instead of their God-given gender at birth. We celebrate these lifestyles rather than teach how they contradict the will of God. Tolerance is not love. Love is having a caring concern about people in lifestyles that will bring them judgment.

We have taken Christ out of Christmas and called it "Happy Holidays." We've taken the nativity scene from our courthouse lawns and the Ten Commandments from our courtroom walls. We have taken prayer and discipline out of our schools. We have terrorists and lone gunmen mowing down innocent people with assault rifles and vehicles. We are currently a very divided nation with looming threats from our enemies. And the list goes on and on.

We have suffered several catastrophic hurricanes, tornadoes, droughts, catastrophic floods, and wildfires and epic temperature plunges in the South. The world has suffered a global pandemic with more deadly viruses on the horizon. Could this be God's judgment on an ungodly nation? An ungodly world? I hope not, but it is looking that way.

3. What does 2 Chronicles 7:13–14 say about such events?

4. Why do *you* think natural catastrophic events are taking place?

5. Where do you believe moral responsibility begins?

6. What are the ungodly influences in our society?

In our home?

7. How do you plan to be an agent for change amid these ungodly influences?

8. What did you learn that was new to you, or what stood out to you in this lesson?

Lesson 31

Genesis 6: Flood Warning, Part Three

Read Genesis 6 and pray that God will speak to you through this lesson.

Answer the following questions.

1. Refer to Genesis 2:4–7. How was the earth watered from the time of creation until the time of Noah?

In Genesis 6:13, God tells His friend, Noah, that He plans to destroy the earth. In verse 14, God tells Noah how to prepare for it. Noah and no one else in the world had never seen rain, had never seen a flood, and had never seen a boat!

2. Look at Hebrews 11:7. What was the underlying motivation of Noah's obedience? (King James and the NIV translations have the most accurate translation of this verse.)

3. In your opinion, what are the underlying reasons society and nations become corrupt, evil, and violent?

4. In your own words, what preparations was Noah commanded to make in verses 14–21?

It's estimated by taxonomists that approximately 18,000 species of mammals, birds, reptiles, and amphibians were on the ark. It's also estimated there were probably not more than 35,000 individual vertebrate animals the average size of sheep on the ark. In other words, picture about 522 railroad stock cars full of animals on the ark.

It's possible the youngest of the largest animals like dinosaurs, elephants, and mammoths were brought to the ark so they would be smaller in stature as well as live longest after the flood.

It's interesting to look closely at verse 20. God tells Noah the creatures will come to him! Two things to think about: the earth is a big place. This may have been the beginning of migration for animals because animals sense weather dangers. Up until this point, there is no evidence of weather dangers.

Also, hibernation is an interesting thought. On the ark, these animals were in small places. For about a year they had limited food until the floodwater subsided. Was this the beginning of hibernation? I have no idea, but it is something to ponder. Remember that only eight people were on the ark, and these eight people had to feed all these animals!

Verse 22 tells us Noah did everything God commanded him to do. The world was violent, immoral, and corrupt. No one had ever seen rain and certainly not a flood or a boat. Can you imagine the jokes made of Noah while he built something that didn't make sense to everyone else?

One verse comes to my mind here. Proverbs 3:5 tells us "Trust in the Lord with all your heart and lean not on your own understanding; in all your ways acknowledge him, and he will make your paths straight."

5. What impresses you most about Noah and his obedience during this *120-year* preparation?

6. Can you describe a circumstance in your own life where waiting on God's timing was a challenge?

What did you focus on during that challenging time that gave you encouragement?

7. According to Luke 17:26–29, what were people doing the day God brought His judgment on the whole earth and then later to the wicked cities of Sodom and Gomorrah?

Today looks much like the days of Noah as well as Sodom and Gomorrah! Some people scoff at the possibility of judgment on our country. Many don't believe we will suffer judgment for the sinful laws we've passed. I think about the lack of wisdom regarding these matters. A verse comes to my mind. Psalm 111:10 says, "The fear of the Lord is the beginning of wisdom." I believe we have become a country that, for the most part, no longer fears God, and we have lost our wisdom.

Only eight people out of the entire planet earth feared God and had the wisdom to believe they deserved judgment. Only eight people got on that ark.

God saw. God warned. Noah prepared.

8. Do you believe your country is on the verge of imminent judgment? If so, how are you preparing for it?

9. If you could plug yourself into this story, which character would you be? God's friend who would hear the warning and be instructed on how to prepare? The family member who was granted a pass to the ark? Or one of many destroyed

by the flood because they didn't have a relationship with the Lord?

"The higher the risk, the greater the return!" Noah risked everything to follow God's warning and instruction. He took a risk and he returned. He returned to dry land!

10. What did you learn that was new to you, or what stood out to you in this lesson?

Lesson 32

Genesis 7:1–10: Get on Board!

Read Genesis 7:1–10 and pray that God will speak to you through this lesson.

Answer the following questions.

I don't know about you, but I am so impressed with Noah's obedience! I've been thinking about the enormous amount of work it took to build an ark that is roughly the size of one-and-a-half football fields! Think about it. Noah didn't have chainsaws to cut the trees. He didn't have a sawmill to cut the lumber. And he didn't have electric tools to construct the ark! Yet for 120 years, he kept at it, trusting that what he was hearing from God would eventually come to pass.

That is exactly the lesson I am aiming at today! God's Word is telling us what will come to pass, and we must prepare ourselves for that coming day. With Noah, God got very specific about how to prepare. He gave plenty of time to prepare. And He gave seven days to get on board. When the day of judgment arrived, God shut the door. Those who didn't believe were left for destruction, and those who did believe were saved.

Remember that Enoch as well as other patriarchs of Noah's time had been preaching to the people. However, people were turning a deaf ear. As the time for the flood neared, the godly men on earth passed away, and Noah was the only righteous man left among the world's population. As pathetic as that sounds, I want to use that point to drive home another point. God still noticed Noah! He was the needle in the haystack, but God knew who he was and where he was!

It's the same for us today. We may feel like we are a needle in a haystack, hidden away in the middle of the world's population. We may feel that our sins, or for that matter, our obedience, goes unnoticed. However, we are quite visible to our all-knowing, ever-present Lord!

1. What does Matthew 24:38–39 with Revelation 1:1–3 tell you about the dangers of biblical illiteracy concerning the end-times and the Second Coming of Christ?

2. Read Ezekiel 14:12–20. What is the main point of this passage concerning our adult children regarding their salvation?

3. Scripture keeps pointing out that Noah was the only righteous man in the world at that time. Why do you think he was able to take his family into the ark with him? (Refer to Ezekiel 14:21–23, Ezekiel 20:43–44, and Genesis 1:28 for insight.)

4. Look at Genesis 7:2–3, where Noah was instructed to bring clean and unclean animals on to the ark. What do the terms "clean" and "unclean" represent according to Leviticus 10:10?

5. Looking ahead to when the flood ended, what were the "clean" animals used for according to Genesis 8:20? (Also look at Exodus 10:25–26.)

6. In Genesis 7:4, after 120 years, God gives one final warning and a time frame of seven days to "get on board" before judgment comes. What speaks to you personally concerning this point, and what might you need to "get on board" about before hard consequences result?

7. What does 2 Peter 3:9 reveal about God's compassion and His justice?

8. What did you learn that was new to you, or what stood out to you in this lesson?

Lesson 33

Genesis 7:11–24: A Time of Preparation

Read Genesis 7:11–24 and pray that God will speak to you through this lesson.

Answer the following questions.

1. For a typical month, what are some of the things written on your calendar at home?

2. Do you believe the Lord keeps a calendar or has specific dates appointed for particular events? Why or why not?

3. In scripture, the number "forty" often represents a time of preparation or testing. For each verse below, do you think it was a time of preparation or a time of testing? Explain your answer.

Noah and his family in Genesis 7:12–24:

Moses receiving the Ten Commandments in Exodus 34:27–32:

The Israelites wandering in the desert in Numbers 14:33–34:

Jesus fasting in the desert in Matthew 4:1–11:

4. Do you think it's possible that times of testing can be times of preparation? Or the other way around—times of preparation can be times of testing? Explain why, and if possible, give a life experience to support your answer.

5. What did you learn that was new to you, or what stood out to you in this lesson?

Lesson 34

Genesis 7: Our Role Is Simple

Read Genesis 7 and pray that God will speak to you through this lesson.

Answer the following questions.

1. According to Genesis 7:16, who bore the burden of those who were not saved?

2. Looking at the story of Noah so far, what are some key principles you have learned concerning your role as a believer?

3. Some people believe the flood was a local flood. What specific proof is given in Genesis 7:17–23 that supports a worldwide catastrophic event?

Have you ever been looking forward to a vacation in paradise or going home after a long trip only to miss your flight? It's just the worst feeling, my friends! If it's ever happened to you then you know that once the plane pulls away from the gate, there is no way you're getting on that plane. There are no do-overs!

When the rain began to fall and God shut the door to the ark, there were no do-overs for the people trying to escape the rising waters. It must have been a terrible sight for Noah and his family. At this point, there was nothing they could do for their friends and relatives but watch in horror as they struggled amid rising waters in the storm.

Scripture seems to make a point that prior to the day the rain came, life had been going on as usual for these folks. It serves as a warning to all of us. We really have no control over future events, and we really don't know when our end will come. Therefore, you have absolutely nothing to lose and everything to gain by being ready!

The one thing that keeps me up at night is the epic problem of biblical illiteracy in this world. If you don't have God's Word in your life, then you won't have a clue of what's ahead, and you will be totally unprepared for it!

I taught Revelation a few years ago, and I'm so thankful I did! It is the only book in the Bible that promises a blessing if you take it to heart (Revelation 1:3). Revelation helps you understand what is in store for those who do not believe but gives great hope and anticipation to those of us who do believe!

There are many parallels between the flood and the Second Coming of Christ. If you are new to Bible study and you don't understand what the Second Coming of Christ is, I will explain it.

First, during Noah's time, there were godly men who taught others about God. However, the world was not listening. People rejected the warnings of the flood and God's judgment on the world. They also rejected the laws of righteous living.

The world became so corrupt, evil, and violent that the only solution at the time was for the Lord to start over by cleansing the earth of all the filth. For 120 years the message was preached, and Noah was building the ark, but no one took it seriously. God's timetable is not our timetable, but His timetable is specific. In Genesis 6:3, God told Noah that He would send a flood in 120 years!

This gave Noah time to build the ark and for the world to come to repentance. Sadly, no one listened, no one responded to the convicting words of the preachers, and no one repented. The ark was finished. God delivered the animals to the ark to be loaded. Then, God gave one last warning siren to get on board. God said that in seven days the floodwaters would come! How disappointing it must have been for Noah and the Lord that not one person outside

Noah's immediate family came to the ark over the course of that week.

The time had come, according to the Lord's calendar, for the rain to come down. 2 Peter 3:8–13 tells us that God is patient, not wanting anyone to perish. However, there is a definite end to God's patience.

Our world is full of corruption, violence, and evil. Maybe we can turn it around, but it takes all believers to do their part. As in Noah's time, we are expected to share God's Word with others. However, it is not our responsibility if they reject the truth. God closes the door of opportunity to come to Him, not us!

If our country does not repent of the ungodly laws we've passed, and put God back in our schools, on our courtroom walls, and in our government buildings, then our nation is doomed for certain judgment. All through God's Word, there are stories about rebellion and the consequences they faced because of it. The question is, will it just be a national judgment or a judgment of all earth?

As believers, we may witness God's judgment. However, like Noah and his family who found safety in the ark, we can take comfort in our eternal salvation.

1 Thessalonians 4:13–18 is a comforting scripture to believers. It refers to the rapture of all believers, those who have previously passed away, and the believers living at the

time of the Second Coming of Christ. We will be caught up to heaven before the judgment of the earth takes place.

The terrible reality is that the Holy Spirit that dwells in every believer will leave the earth, too! Satan will have full reign with no Holy Spirit on earth to hold him back. This will set up the world for seven years of great turmoil and catastrophic events. This seven-year period is known as the great tribulation. It will be a time for unbelievers to get their act together and realize that God is real, and they better get on board with it! This would be the same kind of opportunity to "get on board" as when God gave in His final warning seven days before the floodwaters came.

After the great tribulation, the unbelievers will perish, and the believers will enjoy a thousand years on earth with the Lord as king. This is known as the thousand-year reign.

At the end of the thousand-year reign, Satan will be released, and a final battle will take place between Satan and God. However, God wins! Satan will be destroyed along with his many angels who were cast down with him in the beginning. And *finally*, the earth will be restored back to its original condition as it was in the beginning before sin brought decay and death into the world. There will be a new Jerusalem and we will once again live in the physical presence of God on earth like Adam and Eve did in the Garden of Eden.

Folks, this is a real time that is coming. It is on God's calendar! The Bible is full of prophesy that has been fulfilled to the year, if not to the day, according to historical records. Daniel is one of the most interesting books in the Bible to study because history has unfolded exactly as Nebuchadnezzar's vision and Daniel's interpretation of it foretold. In Daniel 9, the seventy "sevens" unfolded exactly to the timeline they represented.

Once our life on earth ends, or the Lord returns while we are still alive, there will be no do-overs! We will not have another chance to get on board.

I am passionate about Bible study because I was saved in Bible study. I went to church my whole life and even had a prayer life. However, my faith was that of my parents. I believed because my parents believed! So, in other words, my faith was my parent's faith. I didn't really "own" my faith. It wasn't until I sold those silly purses in the church bazaar that God specifically pointed out my sin to me. At that point, I knew the Lord was real! Not because my parents told me He was real, but because I experienced Him firsthand and personally.

Folks, God commanded Noah to put his family on that ark because God knew that when they experienced God's power of judgment that they would believe! Not because Noah believed but because they experienced God firsthand and personally!

I asked you if you thought times of testing were times of preparation and vice versa. Scripture does not mention that God spoke to Noah during the 120 years he was building the ark. That would definitely have been a time of testing for Noah. Sometimes it's hardest to be obedient during times of silence. However, the discipline that comes with that kind of obedience and focus can prepare us for the hardships ahead.

I ask you, sweet friend, are you living life as usual? Or is the Lord changing you each week through these lessons? Is the Lord getting specific with you about how you need to prepare yourself for the day you leave this earth?

Don't get caught up in the floodwaters of the world! Pursue the Lord with all your heart and walk through the open door to salvation.

"For God so loved the world, that he gave his one and only Son, that whoever believes in him shall not perish but have eternal life" (John 3:16).

"Jesus answered, 'I am the truth and the life. No one comes to the Father except through me'" (John 14:6).

Folks, if you struggle with believing that God is real and His Word is truth, pray and ask Him to help you with your unbelief!

I mentioned my parents earlier. They were wonderful parents who took me to church and walked the talk, as people say. They set a godly example for me. Having said that, when death is staring you in the face, it is easy to get scared. I remember my mother being told in the hospital that she probably wouldn't live long with her failing heart valve. I remember her lip trembling as she admitted to me that she was afraid to die. I knew she was a believer. When I reminded her that her body would die but she would continue to live, her eyes lit up and a huge relief came over her.

I watched my mother pass from this life into the next with absolute confidence and peace because she knew the Lord. I even had a precious thing happen once that let me know she was looking down at me. It's too special and private to share, but friends, that is the hope that believers have and share with one another!

How about you? If you knew you were going to die suddenly, do you have peace and confidence about what lies on the other side of this life? Don't be caught on the side of God's judgment. Listen to the Word of God and get on board for salvation's sake!

4. What did you learn that was new to you, or what stood out to you in this lesson?

Lesson 35

Genesis 8: God Remembers Us

Read Genesis 8 and pray that God will speak to you through this lesson.

Answer the following questions.

Folks, I'm in my sixties. I have had a few trying times in my life. I can tell you what year, if not what month, those trials began and ended for me. I noticed with Genesis 8, the days and months were important to Noah, as well. When a person endures something as catastrophic and gut-wrenching as Noah did, you remember the details and the timeline pretty distinctly!

It's easy to speed through a chapter and even speed through a lesson. However, you will miss points to ponder that make these people so relevant. I hope as you answer the following questions, you will really put yourself in Noah's situation. Try to get in his mind at the time and think about things from his perspective. Then, I hope as you go about your week and your life you will remember and reflect on this story. If you do, you might remember there is a light at the end of the dark tunnels in life, and God's timing is so different from ours!

1. After reading Genesis 8, read the following verses. Briefly describe the difficult situation in each group of verses.

Genesis 7:24 and 8:1:

Genesis 19:29:

Exodus 2:23–24:

1 Samuel 1:5–7, 11, and 19–20:

What seems to be a recurring word in each of the scripture verses concerning God?

2. What does 2 Peter 2:4–9 tell us about godly people and their trials?

3. Noah had never seen rain and certainly never a flood. In Genesis 7:4, God tells Noah He will send rain on the earth for forty days and forty nights and wipe the earth clean of all the living. Put yourself in Noah's place. If you had never experienced this sort of catastrophe, how long would you be expecting the flood to last according to what God told Noah in Genesis 7:4?

4. According to Genesis 8:3, how many days had gone by when the waters had gone down?

5. According to Genesis 8:4, what amount of time did it take for the bottom of the ark to even touch or rest on a mountaintop?

6. According to Genesis 8:5, how long was it before the tops of the mountains became visible?

7. The total time it took from the beginning of the first raindrop until Noah was allowed to disembark from the ark was 371 days. In your own words, describe what you think those 371 days were like for Noah physically, mentally, and spiritually.

Janice Bobanis

Physically:

Mentally:

Spiritually:

8. Noah was fully aware of why, when, and how the Lord would cleanse the earth of corruption and evil, yet Noah didn't have a full comprehension of how long it would actually take. What inspires you, encourages you, or challenges you about the length of this process?

9. Is there a situation in your own life where a cleansing of ungodly habits or influences is necessary to restore things back to a more godly form of living? What steps do you need to take to make these changes?

Noah used a raven and then a dove to test the conditions of the flood-ravaged land. The raven, which fed off dead bodies and putrefying flesh, flew back and forth to the ark. It was finding food but no place to make a home. The water was still too high. Then, Noah sent out a dove. After three tries over a period of weeks, the dove produced concrete evidence that the land was dry, and the period of cleansing was over. However, Noah waited for God before he disembarked from the ark.

10. Is there a situation in your own life where you need to see concrete evidence before you know things are right again?

11. What did you learn that was new to you, or what stood out to you in this lesson?

Lesson 36

Genesis 8: Reverent Perspective

Read Genesis 8 and pray that God will speak to you through this lesson.

Answer the following questions.

1. Compare Genesis 1:20–28 with Genesis 8:15–17. Then read Isaiah 14:24–27. According to these verses, do you think God's will can be thwarted? Explain.

2. What does Noah do after he disembarks from the ark, and how does the Lord react to it according to Genesis 8:20–22?

The burnt offerings mentioned in Leviticus 16:8–13, 8:18–21, and 16:24 were a form of worship to God. A bull, ram, or male bird (dove or young pigeon) was to be without defect and completely burned to ashes. This was a voluntary act of worship, atonement for unintentional sin in general, and an expression of devotion, commitment, and complete surrender to God.

3. Look closely at Genesis 8:21. At what point in our lives are our hearts inclined toward evil?

We are born with a sinful nature. We must recognize our sin, come to Jesus Christ, and understand we need His sacrifice on the cross to be reconciled to God. From that point on, we are no longer controlled by the sinful nature, but by the Holy Spirit that comes to live within our hearts. We will still sin. However, it will not control us.

Many people have things backward in their minds. We don't come to Jesus when we are clean enough. We come to Jesus because we are dirty with sin. He has already shed His blood. That blood cleanses us, and He forgives us. We then have access to God, and He hears our prayers.

We are a work in progress. We come to Jesus, He cleanses us, and then He grooms us for eternal life. Through His Word (scripture), He teaches us, convicts us of sins we need to let go of, and grooms us into a holy, godly person.

4. What moves you about Noah's worship after he endured such a difficult journey?

5. What stands out to you the most concerning the flood and Noah's role in it, and how does it apply to you?

6. Looking at Genesis 8:20–22, what do you think this "cleansing of the earth" was like for God?

Now that we have worked through these questions as if we had endured the flood ourselves, let's have some fun with a little trivia. Then we'll get serious again!

Noah's ark came to rest on the mountains of Ararat. Ararat is a high plateau on the far east border of what is now modern-day Turkey. Two peaks rise from this plateau. One peak is called Great Ararat, which is 17,000 feet above sea level. The other is Little Ararat, which stands 13,000 feet above sea level. This gives you a little better perspective of how high the flood waters got!

Since World War II, several expeditions have explored in this region looking for Noah's ark. This area is near the border of Russia. The Russians hampered archaeologists' efforts due to their suspicions of spying! A large wooden structure has been found encased in ice on Mount Ararat. However, the carbon 14 method of testing has come back inconclusive as to whether it is old enough to be the ark.

Speaking of old, Noah lived 950 years! He still had 350 years of life after the flood. I know we've all had those talks about our grandparents and the elderly people we know. My siblings and I have talked about how our grandparents lived during a time of Indian territories and homesteading. They saw transportation go from horseback and buggies to trains, planes, and automobiles. Think about how much the world changed in 950 years!

I am looking so forward to eternal life with people like Noah and Moses! Can you imagine how interesting a dinner conversation could be? Have you ever thought about that? We have so much to look forward to as believers! There will come that day when believers living today will get to meet the people we've studied in our Bible studies.

Jesus tells us in John 14:2, "In my Father's house are many rooms; if it were not so, I would have told you. I am going there to prepare a place for you." This verse has always interested me. I happen to love cooking on a gas stove! I also love lots of clay pots on my patio with flowers and ferns cascading down from them. Is my room going to have a gas stove while Moses has an outdoor pizza oven? Does this eat away at your brain like it does mine? Will I be wearing jeans and a sweatshirt while Abraham is wearing a robe and sash with leather sandals? It really is going to be exciting on the other side of this life! I can't wait to find out these thoughts I've pondered over the years.

Back to a more serious tone. We do still live here on earth where things are not perfect. In fact, they are very far from perfect. Sometimes cleansing is necessary to get things back in sync with God's will. Sometimes, the cleansing has to take place in another person close to us. And sometimes the cleansing needs to take place in ourselves. Whatever the case may be, the journey through it is difficult.

Noah was told it would rain for forty days and forty nights. As I put myself in Noah's sandals, I know I would have struggled with the length of time it took for the whole ordeal to be over. I probably would have expected things to be back to normal after forty days. But we know that wasn't the case. It was much longer and harder than Noah could have possibly imagined.

We've all been through trials that lasted longer than expected. We've prayed and prayed with no evidence the prayers would be answered. But one thing is for sure: God remembered Noah and He remembers you! We just have to remember God's timetable is different from our own.

James 1:2–4 tells us, "Consider it pure joy, my brothers, whenever you face trials of many kinds, because you know that the testing of your faith develops perseverance. Perseverance must finish its work so that you may be mature and complete, not lacking anything."

The term "remembered" in Hebrew means, "began again to act on their behalf." There is a divine purpose for every kind of trial. It may be to cleanse us, or it may be to let us mature and complete our Christian character. We know

God remembers us during those trials. Question is, do we remember God when we get our feet back on dry land?

7. What did you learn that was new to you, or what stood out to you in this lesson?

Lesson 37

Genesis 9: God's Covenant with Noah

Read Genesis 9 and pray that God will speak to you through this lesson.

Answer the following questions.

Our study of Noah is about to come to a close, my friends. There has been so much to admire in Noah: his steadfastness throughout the 120 years of building an ark that no one thought he would use and a year of navigating treacherous floodwaters and watching his friends and relatives wash away. His faith through all of it never failed. Unfortunately, though, it comes to a disappointing end as we watch a spiritual giant like Noah let his guard down, only to be exposed by Ham.

It is not uncommon for people to falter after a great spiritual victory. Moses had successfully led the Israelites out of Egyptian slavery, yet he was a coward when it came to entering the Promised Land. David committed adultery and premeditated murder after he became God's anointed king. The people we study about are just as human as we are. I assume that is the point the Lord wants to make with scripture! The Lord teaches us through the examples of others.

We are all sinners. However, what separates one sinner from another is salvation. Romans 3:22–26 tells us "This righteousness from God comes through faith in Jesus Christ to all who believe. There is no difference, for all have sinned and fall short of the glory of God, and are justified freely by his grace through the redemption that came by Jesus Christ. God presented him as a sacrifice of atonement, through faith in his blood. He did this to demonstrate his justice at the present time, so as to be just and the one who justifies those who have faith in Jesus."

You see, Noah was a righteous man even though he got drunk on wine, passed out, and was found naked in his tent that night. Was the Lord pleased with Noah? Absolutely not! Drunkenness, or any other sin, damages our godly example to others. Noah was considered a righteous man and is even found in the "faith hall of fame" in Hebrews 11. God doesn't desire perfection because perfection is not possible. He wants our devotion. Noah was justified by his faith. I once heard someone put it in simple words. "Justified" means *"just if I'd never sinned."*

So friends, confess your sins but don't allow people to beat you up over them. The Lord forgives you when you put your faith in the blood of Jesus Christ who died to save you!

Christ's blood covers your shame, and you don't have to be chained to past sins any longer!

That being said, let's answer the lesson questions.

1. Genesis 9:1–3, God repeats the same command He gave Adam and Eve: be fruitful, increase in number, and fill the earth. Write the definition for *fruitful* as it applies to Noah and his family in the way they should conduct themselves. (Refer to John 15:1–8 for added insight.)

2. Describe an area of your life where you know you are being fruitful and an area of your life where you need to be more fruitful.

3. Look at Genesis 9:2–3. For what practical reason do you suppose God made the wild animals react this way to Noah and the other seven survivors?

4. Read Genesis 4 and Leviticus 17:11. What was the blood of an animal used for in the Old Testament times according to Leviticus?

5. Write the definition for *atonement*.

6. Look at Deuteronomy 12:16 with John 19:33–34. What do these scriptures have in common?

The red fluid circulating in the bodies of animals and humans signifies the "life" principle in the Old Testament (Genesis 9:4; Leviticus 17:11; Deuteronomy 12:23). Because "the life is in the blood," the Old Testament forbade eating blood or bloody meat (Leviticus 3:17; Deuteronomy 12:16). In the Old Testament times, it was the "life" of the animal that reconciled a sinful human back to God. In the New Testament, it is the "life of Christ" that reconciles a sinful human back to God. The body was sacrificed, and the blood was the cleansing agent for sin.

Read Genesis 9:8–17.

7. A covenant is an agreement between two or more persons in which the following four factors or elements are present: parties, conditions, results, and security.

What parties are involved in the Noahic covenant according to Genesis 9:13?

What conditions were the covenant based on according to Genesis 9:1 and 7?

What results would be fulfilled if the above conditions were met according to Genesis 9:11 and 15?

What security would the people on earth have according to Genesis 9:12–17?

8. Where do you see the rainbow appear according to the following verses?

Ezekiel 1:28:

Revelation 4:2–3:

Revelation 10:1:

I don't know anyone who doesn't enjoy seeing a beautiful rainbow in the sky! I hope when you look up and see one next time, you will not only see God's awesomeness, but you will feel it also!

I hope you will be reminded that He remembers you, sweet friend, just as He remembers His covenant with earth.

9. What did you learn that was new to you, or what stood out to you in this lesson?

Lesson 38

Genesis 9:18–29: Handling Another's Sin

Read Genesis 9:18–29 and pray that God will speak to you through this lesson.

Answer the following questions.

This is where Noah's story takes a disappointing turn. After the flood, Noah became a farmer and planted himself a vineyard. He drank the wine he produced and found himself in a drunken stupor. The definition of stupor is "to descend from one's level of dignity!" I'm sure you would agree that Noah was a dignified, godly, and faithful man. Therefore, I want to make a point here. We should never "worship" people and make them "idols" in our lives because all people, even the most godly, will eventually disappoint us at some point in our lives.

I remember a time when I heard a woman say her faith was shaken because a pastor of her church was accused of sexual misconduct with office staff. The problem was her faith was in the man and not the Lord. Friends, if your faith and devotion to the Lord is dependent on how other Christians act, then you have no real faith. You have placed your faith in the shakable and imperfect qualities of humans rather than the steadfast, unshakable power of God!

Another point I want to address is the controversial subject of drinking among Christians. The Bible is pretty clear concerning this subject. Scripture does not condemn drinking but is clear about the sin of drunkenness. Some people claim that wine was not fermented in biblical times, but this simply is not true. Wine in biblical times contained alcohol just as wine does today. This was as much a part of life then as it is today.

People have their opinions about drinking, but none of them really matter because only what scripture says about it matters! Matthew 11:18–19 shows the contrast between John the Baptist and Jesus. Jesus is addressing a crowd and says, "For John came neither eating or drinking, and they say, 'He has a demon.' The Son of Man (Jesus) came eating and drinking, and they say, 'Here is a glutton and a drunkard, a friend of tax collectors and of sinners.' But wisdom is proved right by her actions."

Well, of course we know Jesus was not a drunkard because He was without sin. He was God in the flesh. Jesus was making the point in Matthew that some people are always looking for fault! My best advice to you is live your life free from legalism and live according to what scripture dictates. You will be a pleasing soul to the Lord even while others are criticizing the way you live.

Janice Bobanis

John the Baptist was a Nazarite and was not allowed to take part in the fruit of the vine because that was the vow he made when he became a Naza*rite.* However, Jesus (a Naza*rene* from Nazareth) possibly did drink wine because he was not under that vow. So the point is, it is not a matter of whether you drink or not; it is a matter of how much!

This is a subject that hits very close to home for me as my husband and I love to cook, we love fine wine, and we entertain guests often. Therefore, my husband always prefaces an evening with guests by saying "It is my job to be a gracious host and your job to manage your glass!"

I will leave this subject with that marvelous quote lingering in your ears. If you cannot manage your glass, then do not partake of the vine!

1. In Genesis 9:20–24, why did Ham not handle Noah's condition appropriately?

2. What were the specific curses and blessings for each son according to Genesis 9:25–27?

Ham:

Shem:

Japheth:

3. What do Joshua 9:23 and Judges 1:28 say about how Ham's curse was fulfilled?

4. As you scroll through the genealogy of Luke 3:23–38, what important person came from the lineage of Shem? (Refer to verses 23 and 36.)

Name four or five other important people in Shem's lineage that you find in these verses.

There are many speculations among scholars as to why Canaan (Ham's son) was the one cursed instead of Ham. One theory is that prophesy would prove him to be more immoral than Ham. The other theory is that somehow Canaan might have been involved because "son" (verse 24) many times refers to "grandson" in scripture. There are other theories, but these theories don't change the fact that Canaan received the curse for his father.

The word "saw" in Genesis 9:22 actually means "gazed upon." Ham and Noah were family, but we know that something evil had transpired in Ham when he "gazed upon" his father. Ham's son received a curse while the other brothers received a blessing. How we respond to others when they fall from grace can be as consequential as it is for the one who falls. Proverbs 24:17 warns us, "Do not gloat when your enemy falls; when he stumbles, do not let your heart rejoice, or the Lord will see and disapprove and turn his wrath away from him."

If we are delighted when our enemies fall, think about how devastating the consequences would be for gloating when *family* falls. Ham experienced that consequence firsthand!

I want to give you a brief, condensed overview of the three brothers, Shem, Ham, and Japheth, and what transpires in their future. We will study about this more in depth in the next lessons when we study the Tower of Babel and Table of Nations.

Shem. They are the Israelites. We will primarily focus on this clan while in the Old Testament. Shem had a son, Arphaxad, the ancestor of Abraham from whom came the Messiah. The three great monotheistic religions of the world (Judaism, Christianity, and Islam) have come through the clan of Shem.

Ham. We will study the ancestor of all the "ites" in future lessons. These people had gross, sensual polytheistic religious practices that included worshipping gods of fertility and temple prostitution. Ham was the father of the following nations: the Hamitic people: Ethiopians, Egyptians, Canaanites, Philistines, Babylonians, and possibly the African and Oriental peoples. Many of the scholars view the Orientals as Japhetic.

Japheth. He was the father of some fourteen nations forming the Indo-Germanic family. His descendants erected the civilizations of the Medo-Persians, produced the Ionians of western Asia Minor, Cappadocians (including the Hittites), Cimmerians, Scythiansm, and the Island Kingdoms of the Aegean. This is significant because the Ionians were one of the four divisions of the prehistoric Greeks who invaded the Greek mainland and, after the Dorian invasions, emigrated to the Aegean Islands and the coast of Asia Minor. At the time of the flood, Japheth was married but had no children.

Because of the Greek invasions, the Greek language became the worldwide language. The Lord was using all of this so the gospel could be spread over the world. With one primary language, the gospel would spread faster.

After the crucifixion of Christ, Paul later became converted from Judaism to Christianity. He took the gospel to the Gentiles first in Asia Minor and then to Macedonia. The Japhetic people heard the gospel when they came to the "tents" of Shem! The blessing of Japheth was essentially a religious one. The Japhetic peoples were the Medes, Greeks, Cypriots, etc., and probably the Caucasian people of Europe and northern Asia.

Most scholars would include the Orientals here.

Now that you have a little ammunition to help you understand future lessons, let's close with a couple of points. First, I want to talk about Noah's vulnerability. We are all vulnerable to stumbling and falling, and Noah was no different. Satan is most likely to tempt you to stumble and fall when you are hungry, angry, lonely, or tired. Noah was definitely tired! So, HALT. Be aware that you are vulnerable!

Remember:

Hungry

Angry

Lonely

Tired

In closing, I want to share an illustration the Lord gave me one morning. The threshold of a doorway can sometimes be a little higher than normal. I want you to imagine it as the area in your life where you are vulnerable to stumbling or even falling. Know where the threshold is. You will be less likely to stumble and fall.

As Christians, our threshold is a little higher than most. People are watching us. Some are even waiting for us to stumble and fall, so be careful. Navigate wisely. None of us would want to "descend from our level of dignity"!

5. What did you learn that was new to you, or what stood out to you in this lesson?

Lesson 39

Genesis 11: God's Plan Cannot Be Thwarted!

Read Genesis 11 and pray that God will speak to you through this lesson.

Answer the following questions.

Friends, we are coming to a stopping point in Genesis with our study of the Tower of Babel and the Table of Nations. It so happens that Genesis 11 chronologically occurs before Genesis 10. The Tower of Babel (chapter 11) is in the process of being built, and then the people are scattered, resulting in the Table of Nations (chapter 10). Therefore, that is how we will study them. Interestingly enough, the story of Job occurs chronologically after the scattering of people in Genesis 11.

Read Genesis 11:1–9 first.

I remember when my children were entering junior high school; it was a new chapter in their lives. I warned them they would see a division among their friends, and we would see a division among parent friends. Some kids would stay on the straight, responsible path and maintain a respect for authority. Other kids, however, would veer off to another path paved with poor choices, rebellion, and a lack of respect for authority. Some parents would choose to be "parents" while others would act like "cool" friends. If you are a parent of teenagers, you know what I'm talking about.

Noah's three sons were no exception, as their descendants chose different paths. When the flood was over and the people on earth began to populate, the families and descendants of Shem, Ham, and Japheth began to migrate from the region of Ararat where the ark had come to rest. At this time, there was only one language among the people: Hebrew. They were united in a common language and for the most part, united in the attitude of living under God's authority.

When they reached the fertile area of Shinar between the two great rivers, the Euphrates and the Tigris, most of them settled there. Shinar was located fifty-nine miles southwest of present-day Baghdad. They made plans to build a great tower and wanted to make a name for themselves. This tower would be very similar to what a pyramid looks like. It would have a large base and taper with each layer toward the top of the tower.

The soil in this area was great for making brick. The soil also contained bitumen, which bubbled up from the ground. This was a mixture of naturally occurring hydrocarbons such as crude petroleum, asphalt, and tar. This substance was used as the mortar to hold the bricks in place. Most of the time, they made sun-dried bricks, but this time they wanted stronger, more durable bricks. Therefore, they baked these bricks in a kiln. These bricks were approximately one square foot and three to four inches thick. They could be brilliantly glazed and arranged in decorative pictorial friezes.

It isn't clear whether Shem's descendants settled in Shinar or moved on. We will talk about why later.

1. In Genesis 11:4, what two clues tell us these people were going down the wrong path? (Refer to God's command in Genesis 9:1.)

2. Can you think of an example in your own life when you knew people were pushing God's will aside to make a name for themselves?

3. Can you think of a time God scattered people because they were unified in achieving something that might not have been God's will?

4. Read Genesis 11:5–7. According to the following verses below, what are some other times in Old Testament days

when the Lord found it necessary to "come down" and take care of business?

Genesis 18:20–21:

Exodus 3:1–10:

Exodus 19:9:

5. What do these verses say about how interested and involved God actually is with humankind, and how does this comfort you regarding a situation in your own life?

Humans cannot thwart God; however, God can thwart humans! In verse 7, the Lord comes down and confuses the language to stop the building of the tower. For the first time in history, there was a language barrier among the people.

6. When have you experienced a situation where God thwarted your plans because it went against His will or plan for your life? What transpired, and how did you realize it was a divine intervention by God?

7. What do the following verses say regarding your plans versus God's plans?

Job 42:1–6:

Psalm 33:11:

Proverbs 16:9:

Which of the above verses speak to you the most, and how do you need to apply it to your own life right now?

8. How do the following verses encourage you about trusting and obeying God?

Psalm 1:1–3:

Proverbs 13:21:

9. Looking at Genesis 11, it is obvious there is great momentum when people are unified. Can you think of a

time when momentum through unity resulted in something destructive?

How about something really great?

The definition for *babel* is a "confused mixture of sounds or voices/a scene of noise and confusion." As you know, it's almost impossible to get anything done when there is a language barrier between people. For the first time in these people's lives, they could not communicate as one people. It is at this time that our different languages were formed. Because the building of the tower couldn't continue, and no one could understand one another, people began to scatter. God had thwarted the very purpose for which they had chosen to live there.

God saw that these people were unified in their purpose and their purpose was in direct defiance of God's command to fill the earth and be fruitful. Out of pride, they wanted to make a name for themselves rather than depend on God and give Him the glory for what they accomplished along the way.

This leads us to the next part of our lesson. When the people scattered, they stayed together within their family units. These units were later known as tribes. Each tribe had their own unique language. It's possible that Shem's descendants had kept moving and never settled in Shinar because the Hebrew language remained intact within the family line of Shem.

As I was preparing this lesson, I came across a very interesting explanation for why there are different skin colors and physical features that differentiate ethic groups. Henry M. Morris is a well-known creationist scientist and bible scholar. In his book, *The Genesis Record,* he explains this.

> As each family and tribal unit migrated away from Babel, not only did they develop a distinctive culture, but also they each developed distinctive physical and biological characteristics. Since they could communicate only with members of their own family unit, there was no further possibility of marrying outside the family. Hence, it was necessary to establish new families composed of very close relatives, for several generations at least. It is well established genetically that variations take place very quickly in a small inbreeding population but only very slowly in a large interbreeding. In the latter, only the dominant genes will find common expression in the outward physical characteristics of the population, reflecting more or less average characteristics, even though the genetic factors for specifically distinctive characteristics are latent in the gene pool of the population.

In a small population, however, the particular suite of genes that may be present in its members, though recessive in the larger population, will have opportunity to become openly expressed and even dominant in these circumstances. Thus, in a very few generations of such inbreeding, distinctive characteristics of skin color, height, hair texture, facial features, temperament, environmental adjustment, and others, could come to be associated with particular tribes and nations. Since earth's population was still relatively young and since, before the Flood, there had been a minimum of environmental radiations to produce genetic mutations, there was yet no genetic danger from inbreeding. After many further centuries had elapsed, however, the accumulation of mutations and the associated danger of congenital defects had become sufficiently serious to cause God to declare incestuous marriages illegal (Leviticus 18:6–14).

It is true that the above sequence of post-Babel events is not actually recorded in Scripture, but it does seem to fit all the real data in science as well as in the Bible.

It is a striking commentary on the importance of human language to note that worldwide migrations and the development of distinct tribes and nations - even their distinctive physical characteristics - were a direct result of the divine imposition of different languages.

As time went on, of course, people found they could, by diligent effort, learn each other's languages. The confounding of languages applied only to the phonologies, not to the underlying thought process, which are part of man's uniqueness. Mankind was still one kind, even though he now was divided into "tongues, in their lands after their nations" (Genesis 10:31). Eventually this would permit a degree of intermarriage and mixing of nations, but the institution of distinct nations became permanent.

It's pretty interesting to know that the Tower of Babel and the scattering of people resulted in our different languages, skin colors, and ethnic diversity! As we move backward in chapter number yet forward chronologically, there is more to learn from the Table of Nations and the historical significances that lie within Genesis 10 and 11:10–32.

10. What did you learn that was new to you, or what stood out to you in this lesson?

Lesson 40

Genesis 10 and 11:10–32: Academic Business

Read Genesis 10 and 11:10–32 and pray that God will speak to you through this lesson.

Answer the following questions.

This is certainly going to be a more academic lesson, rather than a lesson full of life application. However, it is important to learn the historical event of Babel, Noah's genealogy, and the geographical destinations of his descendants so the rest of the Bible can come to life. When we get into further events, you will better understand the dynamics behind the stories.

One interesting note: Noah was living at the time of the scattering. It is likely his son, Shem, who recorded the genealogy of Noah's sons and their descendants. Interesting enough, there are only three generations recorded for Japheth and Ham, while there are six recorded for Shem.

Possibly Shem lost touch with his brothers after a time, and therefore, Shem recorded no further record of their descendants.

Shem lived 502 years after the flood. He was the one most interested in God's promise of the coming seed. In fact, it is through Shem's descendants that the Messiah, Jesus Christ, would be born.

In my research and process of gathering information, I often use Henry M. Morris's *The Genesis Record*. According to name studies and research, he associates Noah's descendants with the following most likely geographical areas they came to represent:

The sons of Japheth (Genesis 10:2–5)

Gomer and his descendants likely settled in Germany, Wales, Denmark, Armenia, and possibly Turkey and the Turkestan area.

Magog and his descendants likely settled in Georgia (a region near the Black Sea). Magog not only settled in Georgia but also in Russia with two other brothers, Meshech and Tubal, and their descendants. (Magog is mentioned in Ezekiel 38:2, 39:6 and Revelation 20:8.)

Madai was ancestor to the Medes, and also merged with Shem's son Elam's descendants and formed the Persian Empire (present-day Iran). Eventually this group of Japhethites developed into the Aryans, who later migrated into India to become the Indian people.

Javans, along with his father, Japheth, is the original founder of the Greeks. Also, Javan's descendants possibly settled in

Spain and Northern Africa in the earliest of days, as well as Italy and the Balkans.

Basically, the descendants of Japheth spread all over Europe, with a main thread of people heading eastward toward Persia and India.

Keep in mind that some of the above geographical calculations are uncertain. However, for the most part, they make logical sense based on research given in these names. An important note to tuck away and remember later is the term "Gentiles." This term was applied primarily to this group of people.

The sons of Ham (Genesis 10:6–20)

Cush migrated first into Arabia and later across the Red Sea into Ethiopia.

Mizraim is ancestor to the Egyptians. Egypt is known as the "land of Ham" (referred to in Psalm 105:23).

Put migrated to Libya, which is in North Africa and west of Egypt.

Canaan was the ancestor to the Canaanites and of course settled in the Land of Canaan. Many Bible-study students simply refer to Canaan's descendants as the "ites" of the Land of Canaan. These "ites" (Hittites, Amorites, etc.) of course will be an important part of our study of Exodus further down the road.

Cush's descendants migrated to Sudan and Arabia. However, one infamous descendant, Nimrod, remained in the Euphrates and Tigris Valley while everyone else scattered. Nimrod means "let us rebel"!

It is believed that Cush, brother to Canaan who received a curse after exposing Noah's drunken episode, was so bitter that he groomed his son Nimrod to lead a rebellion against God's purpose for humankind. Nimrod became a very influential leader and powerful hunter. He gained a substantial following and led a movement in rebellion against God. Nimrod developed a complex of cities, with his kingdom centered in Babylon. He later went forth into Assyria and developed more cities, one of which was Nineveh. Nineveh, as you may recall, was the city that God commanded Jonah to go and preach to.

It is also believed that the descendants of Ham later spread out more than anyone else. This extended area is believed to include current-day China as well as North America and South America via a land bridge over the Bering Sea that existed at one time.

The sons of Shem (Genesis 10:21–32)

Elam was ancestor of the Elamites who invaded the Canaanites during the time of Abram in Genesis 14:4–5. The Elamites later merged with other tribes, especially the Medes (descendants of Japheth) to form the Persian Empire.

Asshur was the founder of Assyria, which later was invaded by Nimrod who developed the city of Nineveh, which later became the capital city. Therefore, the Assyrian people became a mixture of Semitic and Hamitic culture, language, and religion.

Arphaxad was a direct family line to Abraham and the promised seed, Jesus Christ.

Lud does not have much recorded about him.

Aram was the father of the Aramaeans, the same as the Syrians. These people became a great nation. Their language (Aramaic) was adopted as a major language spoken at that time, even among Jews at the time of Christ.

It's interesting to note that Eber, Shem's son, had two sons, Peleg and Joktan. Peleg actually means "divided." The earth is referred to in verse 25 as "divided." Whether this means a division of Gentiles and Jews, a division of people into different nations, or a division of land because of the flood, we don't know exactly. But it is an interesting thought to ponder!

All in all, there ended up being a total of seventy nations that resulted from the confusion of language at Babel. From Shem came twenty-six nations, thirty for Ham, and only fourteen for Japheth.

What most people tend to skip over while studying the Bible actually becomes the very nugget of information that brings everything into focus. On the surface, the Table of Nations doesn't seem too interesting, but we have learned many things from this study. We know how the different languages formed and we know why different skin colors and physical features are common among different nationalities. We also see this as a time when two distinct groups are just beginning to emerge from Noah's three sons: the Jews and the Gentiles.

We have gotten a little lost in the Table of Nations, but let's revisit the Tower of Babel for a minute. As one people, they settled in Shinar. They defied God's command to fill the earth, and they wanted to make a name for themselves. This was a unified anti-God movement that wanted to be in charge of their own destiny. It is believed the only people who were not really on board were Shem and his descendants. The reason this is probable is because the Hebrew language remained intact with Shem and his descendants.

As I said at the beginning of this lesson, a division was occurring among these people; the true followers and those who chose a path paved with poor decisions because they wanted to make a name for themselves.

It's easy to want to do what is comfortable. These people wanted to all stay together. They thought they could reach heaven by their own works. But the Lord calls us to step out of our comfort zone, depend on Him for direction, and give Him the glory!

1. What did you find interesting about the commentary above?

2. Where might you be compromising God's plan for your life because you prefer to stay in your comfort zone or even make a name for yourself?

3. What do you fear most about stepping out of your comfort zone? What are you going to do about it?

4. What has inspired you, convicted you, or taught you the most in these lessons?

If you know your Bible, then think about what happens to these groups of people. Japheth, Ham, and their descendants fell into the worship of created things. This all began when they believed that a tall tower built to the heavens could do more for them than what God could do for them. But for Shem, his obedience would be blessed. His descendants would inherit the very land in which Canaan, Ham's son, would settle.

As we move forward in the next volume of this Genesis study, we'll see God set His plans in motion for the true believers and followers! They will eventually inherit a land flowing with milk and honey. Shem's descendant,

Abraham, would be promised this land. Thus, the land of Canaan is called the "Promised Land." This is our current nation of Israel. It will also be the center of worship when Christ returns and sets up His kingdom on earth.

Folks, God has a great plan for each of us. His plans are way beyond our wildest dreams! So, we all need to remember to stay on track with the Lord. We never know what blessings He has in store for us. If you find that you have taken a detour, get back to where you need to be, and He will lead you to a blessing!

5. Are you settled in a place that might not be God's will for your life? What first step are you going to take to get on track?

6. What did you learn that was new to you, or what stood out to you in this lesson?

7. After tackling forty lessons on the first eleven chapters of Genesis, what is the most impressive thing you have learned overall?

8. Overall, what have you applied from these lessons that has changed your life the most?

Friend, thank you for investing the time to do these lessons. I hope they have blessed you. I hope they have enriched the way you go about your life. And most of all, I hope you have found a special friend in Jesus. May you find Him a comforting companion on your life's journey!

Please join me for the next study in this Genesis series, *A Lot to Handle.*

Author's Resources

Notes

1. Henry M. Morris. *The Genesis Record* (California: Creation-Life Publishers, 1976), 17–290

Bibliography

McDonald, William. *Believer's Bible Commentary.* Tennessee:Thomas Nelson Publishers, Inc, 1995.

Morris, Henry M. *The Genesis Record: A Scientific and Devotional Commentary on the Book of Beginnings.* California: Creation-Life Publishers, 1976.

Pfeiffer, Charles F. and Howard F. Vos, John Rea. *Wycliffe Bible Dictionary.* Massachusetts: Hendrickson Publishers, Inc, 2001.

The NIV Classic Reference Bible. Michigan: The Zondervan Corporation, 1988.

Today's Parallel Bible NIV, NASB, KJV, NLT
Michigan: The Zondervan Corporation, 2000.

Zondervan Handbook to the Bible. Michigan: Zondervan
Publishing House, 1999.

Printed in the United States
by Baker & Taylor Publisher Services